TRUSTEE HANDBOOK

A Guide to Effective Governance for Independent School Boards

Seventh Edition

by Mary Hundley DeKuyper

National Association of Independent Schools
Suite 1100, 1620 L Street NW, Washington, DC 20036-5695

Reprinted 1998, 2001, 2002

ISBN 0-934338-96-5

Designed by Musikar Design, Rockville, Maryland

ACKNOWLEDGMENTS

I deeply appreciate the National Association of Independent Schools "team" that contributed to this handbook. I particularly want to thank Kathleen (Kiki) Johnson, vice president for institutional leadership, who served as cheerleader and mentor throughout the development of the book. Her advice was critical to the project, and her knowledge informed every chapter. I also want to thank the members of the NAIS Trustees Advisory Committee who shared their perspectives on independent school governance and supported this project from the beginning — and especially Henry L. (Skip) Kotkins, Jr. for his careful reading of the manuscript and insightful suggestions. And thanks goes to the NAIS staff members and executive directors of state associations who assisted in the development of the case studies — and to Michael Brosnan who edited the manuscript.

I thank all those trustees and heads of school with whom I have had the pleasure to work. Their wisdom, commitment to their schools' missions, desire to make a difference in the lives of their students, and deep individual and collective interest in adding value to their boards and schools have enriched and educated me.

I especially thank the remarkable women and men with whom I served as The Bryn Mawr School trustees. My experience on that board was among the most rewarding of all my service on nonprofit boards. I wish every board president or chair the opportunity to experience the dynamic and warm relationship with their head of school as I had with Barbara Landis Chase (head of The Bryn Mawr School 1980-1995 and current head of school at Phillips Academy). She was a valued colleague, a strong, visionary leader, and an educator of girls and young women, trustees, and board presidents par excellence!

— Mary Hundley DeKuyper

CONTENTS

Chapter 1

Principles of Good Practice for
Boards of Trustees and Independent School Trustees

Chapter 2

Keeping the Mission and Serving as Fiduciary of the School

Chapter 3
Developing and Reviewing Policy

Chapter 4
Developing a Shared Vision and Planning Strategically

Chapter 5
Assuring the Financial Strength of the School/Fund-Raising

Chapter 6
Developing the Effective Board

Chapter 7

The Relationship Between the Board and the Head

Chapter 8

The Relationship Between Board Chair and the Head

Chapter 9

Relating to Major Constituencies or Stakeholders

Chapter 10
Organizing an Effective Board

Chapter 11
Performing the Role of Trustees

PREFACE

This new edition of the *Trustee Handbook* is an excellent guide for trustees and heads of independent schools. It is also an expression of thanks and appreciation for the devotion of people who believe in independent education, those willing to give of their time and talents to help our schools be the best they can be. The ability of the school to act independently, even to exist, is based on the foundation of its governance. At the very core, we have determined that effective governance will remain the foundation of the healthy independent school. There is no work more important.

Whether you have many years of experience or are new to the board, the book is intended to help you understand all of your responsibilities as a trustee. It will help you understand the complexities and nature of service on the board, while offering practical and useful information for every aspect of trusteeship. For school heads, the book will help clarify your relationship with the board, especially the board chair, and ultimately help make you a better leader with a better leadership team.

Why a new edition? Circumstances, laws, and needs have changed so much in recent years that we must view trusteeship in entirely new ways. These complex times require fresh perspectives and refined skills. We are learning more every year about the science and craft of trusteeship. This new edition of NAIS's most popular book reflects all that we have learned to date.

A special thanks goes out to Mary DeKuyper, the author of this new *Trustee Handbook*. While the book builds on the past, it adds significantly to our knowledge of what it means to be an effective board member — especially in the areas of strategic planning, the trustees' role in fundraising, and the importance of diversity. This seventh edition also includes the newly revised *NAIS Principles of Good Practice for Independent School Trustees* and the *Principles of Good Practice for Boards of Trustees*. These, along with the author's elaborations on each principle, are worth the price of admission alone.

The good news is that this is an especially exciting and challenging time to be a new trustee on an independent school board. It is only right that we now have this new *Trustee Handbook*, a work of substance and specificity, to provide guidance and assistance to trustees and heads on their journey. Building on the rich traditions and long history of this nation's independent schools, this handbook is the freshest and most modern approach for effective independent school trusteeship as we make the turn into the 21st century.

— Peter D. Relic, president, NAIS
August 1998

INTRODUCTION

What are we doing here? We're reaching for the stars.

— *Christa McAuliffe*

Welcome to the challenging and rewarding world of independent school trusteeship. You have joined with thousands of men and women who care deeply about
the schools they serve — preschools, elementary schools, secondary schools,
K-12 schools, boarding schools, day schools, single-sex schools, coeducational
schools, religiously-affiliated schools, secular schools, schools in the United
States, American schools abroad, schools for children with special abilities,
schools for children with disabilities. The community of independent schools is
diverse, and the trustees who govern these schools have agreed to accept critical
responsibilities as they work to further their schools' missions.

   In order to be an effective trustee and add value to the work of the board
and the school, you need to be informed about all aspects of your school and
about trusteeship. This handbook can be your companion as you examine your
governance role, whether you are a new trustee or a more seasoned one.

The Handbook's audience

The handbook is designed primarily for trustees and heads. Administrators and
faculty, especially those who interact with trustees on committees/task forces,
should also find the book useful for understanding the different roles of board
and staff and the charges for specific committees. Parents and alumnae/i often
serve as trustees or as nonboard committee members, and the handbook can
help them understand their special relationship to the school and to the board.
Consultants to schools in areas of governance, strategic planning, and searches
will also find it helpful.

How to use the Handbook

All the chapters, with the exception of Chapter 1, follow the same format. They include subject matter content and case studies with questions that can lead to conversations among trustees about the issues in each case and, one hopes, to possible solutions to the problems described. Where appropriate, sample forms and resources are included.

One caution on the sample forms: each school is unique, so the forms should be viewed as guides, not as the only way or last word.

Chapter especially for orientation

Chapter 1 contains an overview of individual trustee and corporate board responsibilities, based on the NAIS *Principles of Good Practice for Boards of Trustees* and *Principles of Good Practice for Trustees*. It is excellent for the orientation of new trustees and administrators. Chapters 9 and 11, used together with Chapter 1, provide basic, essential information for all trustees.

Chapters for general board/committee roles

Chapter 2 — keeping the mission and serving as fiduciaries for the school

Chapter 3 — developing and reviewing board policies

Chapter 7 — the relationship between the board and the head

Chapter 9 — relating to other major constituencies or stakeholders

Chapter 10 — organizing an effective board (key committees include executive, finance, investment, audit, buildings and grounds, personnel, financial aid, education, student life, development, strategic planning, trustee, head's advisory committee)

Chapters for specific committees and task forces

Planning: Chapter 4 — developing a shared vision and planning strategically

Fund-raising: Chapter 5 — assuring the financial strength of the school

Committee on Trustees: Chapter 6 — developing the effective board

Chapters for trustees with limited time

Please make the *Trustee Handbook* your own. Use it when you have a specific question, when you are not sure you understand some part of your governance role, or when you want to find new ways to approach a situation that may be confusing. As a trustee, you will find you can be most effective when you con-tinue to learn more about your school and your role as a board member. You are on an exciting journey, along with your fellow trustees. Bon voyage!

Principles of Good Practice for Boards of Trustees and for Independent School Trustees

Good schools have a sense of mission that kids and adults can all articulate. They have an identity. They have a character, a quality that's their own, that feels quite sturdy. They have a set of values.... Good schools are also a disciplined place. I don't mean by that just behavioral discipline, but a place where people set goals and standards and hold each other accountable.

— Sara Lawrence Lightfoot

As an independent school trustee, you have been charged with carrying out very important duties. However, you have not been elevated to a special status; you have not been coronated to serve on the board. You, in partnership with the head, provide leadership and a framework within which the faculty members enact the institutional mission every day as they teach their students.

However, there must be a final authority for the school, and that is the board of trustees on which you serve. The board can act only as one body. No individual trustee, not even the chair, can act for the board, unless the board explicitly authorizes an individual to do so. The board, as a corporate body, and you, as an individual trustee, are legally responsible for the school — for all that it does and does not do. Each trustee is equally liable for every board decision, whether you are present or not when the decision was made.

As a board member, your participation in board deliberations is a critical ingredient in the success of the board and thus of the school.

In the increasingly complicated world of independent schools, boards of trustees, who serve part-time without pay, have delegated to the head the responsibility for administering the school and designing and implementing the curriculum. This delegation is done within the school's mission and broad institutional policies and is subject to the oversight of the board. (More in-depth information on the board's legal or fiduciary duties can be found in Chapter 2. The responsibilities of individual trustees are outlined in Chapter 11.)

Over the years, the National Association of Independent Schools has developed a series of principles of good practice in various key areas of school operation — including principles for boards of trustees and for individual trustees. The principles define high standards and ethical behavior.

The following is an annotated version of NAIS's principles of good practice for a board of trustees and for individuals serving on the board.

Keeping the Mission and Serving as Fiduciaries of the School

Principles for boards

#1 The board prepares a clear statement of the school's mission and objectives.

In creating and reviewing the mission, the board must focus on and understand the unique focus and expertise of the school. It must realize what the school is not as well as what it is. Too many mission statements are almost generic — they could apply to many schools. Boards that truly understand the role of their schools in the communities they serve draft mission statements that, by themselves and without amplification, clearly articulate the vital, inviolate characteristics of these schools. Good mission statements do not explain "how" or "why." They communicate "what" in clear, inspiring, and guiding words.

Mission statements last over time, but regular reviews of the mission are important so that trustees understand and support it. In reviewing a mission statement, it is just as valuable an exercise to intentionally affirm the current wording as to change it. In fact, all strategic planning should begin with the mission statement and end with checking the new plan against the statement.

* As a trustee, you understand the mission, articulate it wherever you are, and use it as a guidepost for making board decisions.

#2 The board reviews and maintains bylaws, and establishes policies and plans consistent with the mission.

The board's internal "rules" are found within its charter, bylaws, and broad institutional policies and plans — all of which should be in concert with the mission. Bylaws should facilitate the work of the board, serve as a reference point for major procedures, and be concise. Bylaws should be reviewed by outside counsel when first drafted and whenever there are substantial changes. If a parliamentary authority is cited (usually Roberts Rules of Order, Newly Revised), board members should have a basic knowledge of parliamentary procedures so that full discussion is encouraged, the rights of the minority are protected, and the majority can come to a decision. The board should establish broad institutional policies, from which the administration can develop operational policies and procedures. Bylaws and broad policies are the basic governance documents of the board.

* As a trustee, you understand the bylaws and seek to be an effective participant in board deliberations, helping to keep board discussions at the policy level.

#11 The board assures compliance with applicable laws and regulations and minimizes exposure to legal action.

The board should establish policies that address actions necessary to reduce risks and require the head to report periodically to the board on risk management actions undertaken. Examples of risk management policies/ procedures are up-to-date personnel policies, appropriate student discipline procedures, and sufficient insurance coverage, including directors and officers liability insurance that covers board members for actions that are not criminal or willfully negligent. To give professional advice in a number of areas, the board should engage outside legal counsel on retainer, to be available to advise the board when the need arises. Attorneys can be valuable trustees, but trustees should not serve as the school's legal counsel. The board needs truly independent advice.

* As a trustee, you assure that the appropriate risk management policies are in place and that you are vigilant in assessing potential risks.

Principles for trustees

#1 A trustee actively supports and promotes the school's mission.

Trustees not only determine the school's mission and set and periodically review the mission statement, they must be able and willing to articulate the mission in formal and informal situations. The school community and the world beyond look to trustees as the people, along with the head, who understand the mission and care deeply about the school. Therefore, each trustee is expected to be an advocate for the mission of the school.

* As a trustee, you are enthusiastic about the school — its mission, faculty, students, curriculum — and such enthusiasm can be very contagious.

#2 A trustee is knowledgeable about the school's mission and goals, as well as current operations and issues.

Trustees need to understand all aspects of the school. They need to be aware of all major issues, and when they are not sure of the facts, they should seek the answers from the appropriate source or sources. However, they need to be sure that the issue at hand is truly a board concern, rather than one for the administration or faculty. When trustees are involved in mission discussions and the setting of institutional goals, they become very effective advocates for the school.

* As a trustee, you are an informed school advocate.

#4 The board sets policy; the administration implements policy. An individual trustee does not become involved in specific management, personnel, or curricular issues.

Trustees are required to be responsible for the school as a whole. As part of this responsibility they set broad institutional policies, within which the administration operates the school. The line between institutional policies and operational policies and procedures is not always as fixed or rigid as was thought in the past. Boards and heads need to establish a climate of trust that encourages candid conversations whenever a question of board policy vs. administrative policy and procedure arises. Trustees need to understand how staff, parent, and student grievances are resolved and how the curriculum is developed. Specific issues in any of these areas are the province of the administration and faculty, and if a trustee is contacted, he or she needs to refer the issue to the head.

* As a trustee, you keep your eye on the big picture and enable the head to run the school.

Fiscal Responsibilities: Stewardship of Resources

Principles for boards

#3 The board is accountable for the financial well-being of the school, including capital assets, operating budgets, fund-raising, and endowment.

The board is organized so that all trustees can be assured that the school's finances are well managed and secure. The board requires periodic reports on the status of all school funds and physical assets, as well as on the financial performance as measured against the budgeted amounts. The board approves the annual budget and requires a yearly independent audit.

* As a trustee, you understand the finances of the school, actively participate in board discussions, and assure that the necessary financial policies are in place.

Principles for trustees

#9 A trustee contributes to the development program of the school, including financial support and active involvement in annual and capital giving.

As a part of assuring the financial well-being of the school, trustees contribute monies to the annual fund and any capital campaign at a leadership level equal to their ability to give. There is an expectation that all board members will make a personal gift to both types of campaigns — and that trustees will demonstrate their support at the beginning of the campaign. A fundamental rule of fund-raising is that you must make your gift before asking anyone else; it is especially important for trustees to do so.

Once trustees have committed to their personal contribution, they need to participate in raising funds from others. The most effective method of soliciting funds is the direct request, but many individuals find this a very difficult task. If some trustees have problems asking for major gifts, training should be provided for them and other fund-raising activities should be offered so that they can use their particular skills and connections. Many schools that hold a number of special events find that their constituents, including trustees, become tapped out. A school should seek to have balanced sources of funds — tuition, annual fund, endowment income, special event income all are important. Trustees need to be sure that the school has a clear, long-term development plan that allows the school to thrive and further its mission.

As a trustee, you will give and get — cheerfully!

#10 Each trustee, as well as the treasurer and finance committee, has fiduciary responsibility to the school for sound financial management.

Every trustee is responsible for the financial well-being of the school and as such must have a basic knowledge of the school's fiscal status. Most boards have a finance committee; others may have a subcommittee or separate committee that oversees and reports on financial activities. This committee cannot make policy nor decide which institutional priorities should be funded. It can tell the board what funds are available, and then turn funding decisions over to the total board, which then set priorities. The board as a whole makes all major funding decisions, such as approving the yearly operating budget, setting tuition, adopting financial policies, and agreeing to undertake a capital campaign and setting its goal.

As a trustee, if you do not understand the finances of the school, you seek to be educated on financial matters and you actively participate in board financial discussions.

The Critical Relationship between Board and Head

Principles for boards

#4 The board selects, supports, and nurtures the head.

The single most important act of a board is the selection of the head. This process should take careful thought, adequate time, and occur only after the school's leadership (board, administration, and faculty) reach consensus on the school's mission and major strengths and concerns. However, once the head has been selected and arrives on campus, the hard work of building and maintaining this special relationship begins. The board needs to support the head in formal and informal ways — paying the head well, keeping the board focused on the big issues and allowing the head to administer the school, being available for advice when sought by the head, etc. Funds should be available to support the head's personal development. Trustees should also offer the head positive as well as negative feedback. (More on this topic in Chapter 7.)

As a trustee, you are committed to keeping the board's relationship with the head a dynamic and positive one.

#5 The board, or a committee of the board, conducts a written annual evaluation of the performance of the head and works with the head to establish goals for the following year.

One of the major ways a board supports the head is to conduct a fair, annual written evaluation of the head's performance. This evaluation should be based on criteria predetermined by the board and the head; it can include personal goals if the head wishes to receive feedback on such goals. It is important that part of the orientation of a new head involves a discussion of the evaluation process and the basis for evaluation during that first year of headship.

Often a subset of the board (executive committee, personnel committee, ad hoc task force) conducts the actual evaluation. Frequently, the board's input is sought by means of an instrument designed for this purpose. Sometimes others beyond the board participate. A smaller group can gather the information and develop the written report, which is then shared with the head by the sub-group, or often just by the chair and one other person. The head is given an opportunity to respond, and the report or a summary of the report is shared orally with the total board in executive session. This is one time that the head is not present. (More on this in Chapter 7.)

As a trustee, you participate in the head's evaluation as appropriate and support the head's personal development in order for him/her to be even more effective.

Principles for trustees

#7 A trustee has the responsibility to support the school and its head and to demonstrate that support within the community.

Trustees need to support the head and the school wherever they find themselves. If trustees have questions or concerns, they should ask the head or board chair about them. Once an issue has been resolved by the head (if it is an operational concern) or by the board (if it is a governance matter), trustees must support the outcome. It is not enough to keep silent about such a decision; a trustee needs to be an active supporter of the resolution. If this support is too difficult and the matter is one of great import or conscience, the trustee needs to leave the board, without damaging the board, the head, and the school. To leave the board is an extraordinary action and should never be done without very careful thought. But to stay and disagree is inevitably damaging.

As a trustee, you must ask questions about major issues and participate in appropriate decisions. You respect and fulfill your private, confidential duties as a trustee to question, to think out loud, and even to criticize if appropriate. But you also respect your public role as a trustee to serve as advocate, defender, and, if necessary, as conduit (but not supporter) of dissent.

#8 Authority is vested in the board as a whole. A trustee who learns of an issue has the obligation to bring it to the head of school, or to the board chair, and must not deal with the situation individually.

Trustees come to the board with a variety of experiences, including special relationships with the school, most often as a parent or alumnae/i or both. A trustee must guard against generalizing from his or her personal situation to that of a much wider group. This is one of the most difficult aspects of being a school trustee, but you need to be careful not to be drawn into a situation where you probably lack full knowledge and over which you have no authority.

As a trustee, you are polite to those who contact you with a concern, but are firm in adhering to your trustee role and refer the person to the head of school or the board chair, whichever is most appropriate.

Board Development: Recruitment, Retention, Recognition, and Assessment of Trustees

Principles for boards

#6 The board evaluates itself annually and establishes goals for the following year.

The board development process begins with the annual assessment of the board. Usually, this is accomplished through written instruments that assist the board in measuring its collective effectiveness and that of individual trustees. The board can establish goals for its own education and training activities based on this evaluation. The committee on trustees, responsible for board development and nominating processes, can use the evaluation to facilitate the recruitment of trustees who will fill identified needs. The assessment can also be used to measure the accomplishment of specific board operational goals and to set new ones for the year ahead. If the board evaluates the performance of the head, it is only appropriate that the board also evaluates its own performance, including the actions it takes regarding annual professional development for the board on the topic of governance in independent schools.

* *As a trustee, you participate in the annual board evaluation with candor.*

#9 The composition of the board reflects a balance of expertise and perspectives needed to achieve the mission of the school.

The committee on trustees involves the board and others in identifying potential trustees who meet established criteria. The committee needs to be sure that the qualifications and qualities of new trustees further the work of the board and the school's mission. Diversity in all of its manifestations should be encouraged and celebrated.

* *As a trustee, you are ever on the watch for potential trustees and bring them to the attention of the committee on trustees.*

#10 The board develops itself through new trustee orientation, ongoing education, and leadership succession planning.

The committee on trustees, in partnership with the board chair and head and based in large measure on the board assessment, should plan a yearly formal board orientation for new trustees. It should also plan annual, ongoing board education and training for all trustees. Most often the head facilitates ongoing educational and training activities, whether about trends in education, fund-raising techniques, or potential legislation that could threaten the school's independence, etc.

It is also vital that the committee plan ongoing programs of professional development for all trustees on the topic of governance, shared roles of board and administration.

The team, consisting of the committee on trustees, board chair, and the head, should plan for board succession so that there is a large "pool" of trustees capable of serving as officers and committee chairs. Potential leaders should be given special training and committee assignments that equip them for future positions.

As a trustee, you seek opportunities for training and education, within and beyond the school, and accept a leadership position, if offered.

Organizing the Effective Board — Adding Value to the School

Principles for trustees

#7 The board keeps full and accurate records of its meetings, committees, and policies.

An effective board keeps its most important records of business (board and committee meeting minutes, budgets and financial reports, institutional policies, bylaws) up-to-date and assures that they are accurate, concise, and timely. Every trustee should have a board manual that contains these items, plus trustee, officer, and committee job descriptions and other documents that would facilitate effective trustee participation in the work of the board.

As a trustee, you make sure all minutes and reports are sent to you before each board meeting. You review them thoroughly and are prepared to ask questions and discuss the issues presented at the meeting.

#8 The board works to ensure all its members are actively involved in the work of the board and its committees.

It is the board, and only the board as a whole, that makes major policy decisions, but it accomplishes its work through committees and task forces. The organizational structure of the board should be as lean as possible and still allow the board to focus on its work. Committees can increase their own effectiveness by including nonboard members from the school and beyond with needed expertise not found on the board. An added benefit from this practice is the opportunity to include potential board members on committees/task forces so that they can be evaluated before asking them to join the board.

* *As a trustee, you are an active member of at least one committee/task force. You work to assure that the board focuses on its own agenda and is organized to do so.*

Conduct of Individual Trustees

All of the topics featured in this chapter so far focus on the board of trustees with implications for individual trustees. Additionally, however, there are three explicit individual trustee principles that need to be highlighted.

Principles for trustees

#3 A trustee attends meetings well prepared and participates fully in all matters.

Just as the board accomplishes its work through committees/task forces, committees/task forces accomplish their work through the efforts of their members. The board itself is only as good as the collective wisdom of the trustees. Thus, trustees need to be informed so they can participate actively and effectively. Materials need to be circulated before meetings in a timely manner. Trustees need to read and understand the material and come prepared to enter into the deliberations.

* *As a trustee, you plan to attend every board meeting and do so, unless there is a real emergency. You prepare in advance, participate fully in the discussions, and facilitate the board's ability to make decisions.*

#5 A trustee accepts and supports board decisions and respects board confidentiality.

The board makes decisions, after opportunities for input and discussion. Sometimes trustees find that they are in the minority on an issue. Even so, they are expected to support the decision outside the boardroom. Supporting decisions you don't agree with is not easy, but such advocacy is critical for successful governance. The understanding and acceptance of the need for public support, after private, confidential discussion — coupled with keeping the confidentiality of board discussions — assures that all trustees will speak with candor during deliberations, that factions will be minimized, and that a climate of trust can be maintained.

* As a trustee, you speak up during board discussions, support the will of the majority, and keep confidential all board deliberations.

#6 A trustee guards against conflict of interest, whether business-related or personal. The trustee takes care to separate the interests of the school from the specific needs of a particular child or constituency.

Trustees may have personal or business-related conflict of interests. This does not mean that they should resign from the board. Their conflicts, however, need to be identified and shared with the board chair. Parent-trustees make up the largest group with the potential conflict centering on their children. For example, parents may view the setting of tuition solely in terms of their own tuition bill. Alumnae/i-trustees may believe that change from the "good old days" is a traitorous act. Of course, the vast majority of trustees do reveal potential or real conflicts and work for the good of the whole school — for today and the future.

* As a trustee, you bring your experience with you to the board table, and you serve as a trustee for the whole school community.

Hot Topics for Board Discussion

As an independent school trustee you follow the *Principles of Good Practice* for school trustees and work to assure the board follows the *Principles of Good Practice* as it fulfills its responsibilities and accomplishes its work of school governance. At the board table what are you discussing, planning for, evaluating? What are the "hot" items about which many trustees are concerned? The following list is not meant to be definitive. Each school has unique concerns, given its mission, size, location, etc. However, there are issues that cut across all types of schools and communities.

◆ Legislation/regulations (local, state, and national) that threaten the independence of independent schools

◆ Financial aid — in what grades should it be offered, full or partial, percentage of budget, merit scholarships, tuition remission, and more

◆ Tuition levels — who can afford the school, the potential loss of middle class families

◆ Diversity — ethnic, racial, gender, and economic diversity of board, administration, faculty, and student body

◆ Sexuality issues

◆ Provision of non-academic services, especially for families and children in stress

◆ Faculty salaries and benefits

◆ Board fund-raising role — all to give at their own highest level

◆ Moving from a mostly parent board to a new design or from a mostly alumnae/i board to a new design

◆ Vouchers and charter schools: funded by public educational funds

◆ Board organization — what committees to have, number of meetings, time of meetings

◆ Governance issues — what is keeping the board from being more effective?

SAMPLE MATERIALS

PRINCIPLES OF GOOD PRACTICE FOR TRUSTEES

The following principles of good practice are set forth to provide a common perspective on the responsibilities of individual members of independent school boards.

1. A trustee actively supports and promotes the school's mission.

2. A trustee is knowledgeable about the school's mission and goals as well as current operations and issues.

3. A trustee attends meetings well prepared and participates fully in all matters.

4. The board sets policy; the administration implements policy. An individual trustee does not become involved in specific management, personnel, or curricular issues.

5. A trustee accepts and supports board decisions and respects board confidentiality.

6. A trustee guards against conflict of interest, whether business-related or personal. The trustee takes care to separate the interests of the school from the specific needs of a particular child or constituency.

7. A trustee has the responsibility to support the school and its head and to demonstrate that support within the community.

8. Authority is vested in the board as a whole. A trustee who learns of an issue has the obligation to bring it to the head of school, or to the board chair, and must not deal with the situation individually.

9. A trustee contributes to the development program of the school, including financial support and active involvement in annual and capital giving.

10. Each trustee, as well as the treasurer and finance committee, has fiduciary responsibility to the school for sound financial management.

PRINCIPLES OF GOOD PRACTICE
FOR BOARDS OF TRUSTEES

The board is the guardian of the school's mission. It is the board's responsibility to ensure that the mission is appropriate, relevant, and vital to the community it serves. The board monitors the success of the school in fulfilling its mission. The following principles of good practice are set forth to provide a common perspective on the responsibilities of independent school boards. The board and the head work in partnership in fulfilling these principles.

1. The board prepares a clear statement of the school's mission and objectives.

2. The board reviews and maintains bylaws, and establishes policies and plans consistent with the mission.

3. The board is accountable for the financial well-being of the school, including capital assets, operating budgets, fundraising and endowments.

4. The board selects, supports, and nurtures the head.

5. The board, or a committee of the board, conducts a written annual evaluation of the performance of the head and works with the head to establish goals for the following year.

6. The board evaluates itself annually and establishes goals for the following year.

7. The board keeps full and accurate records of its meetings, committees, and policies.

8. The board works to ensure all its members are actively involved in the work of the board and its committees.

9. The composition of the board reflects a balance of expertise and perspectives needed to achieve the mission of the school.

10. The board develops itself through new trustee orientation, ongoing education, and leadership succession planning.

11. The board assures compliance with applicable laws and regulations and minimizes exposure to legal action.

CHAPTER TWO

Keeping the Mission and Serving as the Fiduciary of the School

The necessity to educate the board in the techniques and ethical duties of steward-ship cannot be overestimated.

— Art Powell

A s a trustee you are a trustholder for your school. You care deeply for and are committed to your school. You understand your school's char-acter. You uphold your school as it is now, while envisioning what it can be. You are there for your school, and yet not involved in its management. You assure that the school's mission guides all that the school and the board do.

As a trustee, you are legally responsible for the school — as an individual trustee and a member of the board. You make sure that the finances are well managed and secure, that the school obeys all laws and regulations to which it is subject, and that policies and procedures to keep risk as low as possible have been established and regularly reviewed, with appropriate checks and balances for all those who handle funds. It is obvious that neither a board nor individual trustees can manage the day-to-day operations of a school; that is why it hires a professional educator, the head, and she/he in turn hires the professionals who make up the administration, faculty, and other staff. It is through the board's keeping of the mission, setting of broad, institutional policies, and periodic assessment that it assures itself and all stakeholders that the school has in place all that is necessary to protect any school's most precious possession — its integrity.

Trustees as Keepers of the Mission

❖ *What kind of school is this?*

In order to maintain a school's integrity, the school's mission should be the guidepost for all major decisions. The board of trustees is the body that delineates the mission and adopts the statement that describes the mission at the very beginning of the school and reviews both the mission and mission statement periodically. Trustees hold the mission in trust; they are the keepers of the mission. This does not mean that the board sets or reviews the mission in isolation from the rest of the school's community. The board should seek input from administrators, faculty, parents, alumnae/i, and students and then consider these constituent viewpoints during the board's deliberations. However, the final decision to affirm or change the current mission and mission statement rests with the board.

Statement of philosophy

❖ *What is a statement of philosophy?*

Schools often have statements of philosophy which set forth in detail a school's educational beliefs, practices, desires for their students, basic values underlying the school's program, etc. These are usually of some length and are adopted by the board of trustees, just as the board adopts the mission statement. Most often, the faculty and senior administrators, under the head's leadership, draft such a statement.

The mission statement

❖ *What makes a good mission statement?*

Each school is unique, and its mission statement should reflect its uniqueness. During the board's discussion of a mission statement, trustees need to ask, does this statement:

◆ Express the school's reason for being?

◆ Set forth the school's uniqueness and areas of competence?

◆ Reflect the school's philosophy, including its core values and beliefs?

◆ Identify those the school serves?

◆ State the organization's primary strategic direction?

◆ Allow for flexibility in its implementation, while serving as the guide for major decisions?

◆ Set a standard for evaluation of programs and services?

◆ Stimulate energy and commitment?

◆ Read clearly and succinctly?

Few mission statements can fulfill all of the requirements set forth above and be succinct (although there are some excellent exceptions). Boards must balance what is most important for the school at a particular time with a desire for brevity. The shorter the statement, the easier it is for a school community to remember it and for it to inspire action. However, if the words are so brief, non-specific, and generic that they could apply to any school, great confusion could result.

In the board room

The first step any board should take, once they have adopted a mission statement, is to communicate the statement with a rationale, explaining the board's actions. This holds true even when a board has intentionally affirmed the current statement. To assure that the statement "lives," it needs to inform all decisions of the board as well as all other decisions in the school community. It is interesting to note that having a living mission statement assists the board in focusing on governance issues — issues that are broad institutional concerns. You, as a trustee, can add great value to the board's work by asking questions, such as the following:

◆ "Why are we discussing funding a third soccer field when our funds are tight, we cut back on faculty salaries, and our mission stresses the centrality of academics and our commitment to an excellent faculty?"

◆ "Have you thought of the implications of holding a 'slave-auction' fundraiser when our mission stresses our commitment to diversity in all of its forms?"

The school's mission lives daily in the life of the school — within and beyond its walls. A school can stray from its stated mission in major and minor decisions for reasons such as increasing enrollment or garnering more funds. But when this happens, a school can lose its reputation for integrity, and this loss can cripple a school in the long run. Trustees need to be ever vigilant in their role as keepers of the mission.

In the school and broader community

Often, trustees are amazed to discover they are perceived as experts on the school. They do need to be knowledgeable about its program, major strengths and concerns, and, above all, mission. However, it is not enough to understand and support the mission. They need to be articulate, enthusiastic advocates of the mission. Trustees need to be prepared to defend and further the mission in formal and informal settings, be it the parking lot, neighborhood party, or athletic event. If you are uncomfortable with this role, you need to ask yourself why. Do you really support the mission or are you just not used to speaking out? If it is the former, you should resign from the board; if it is the latter, get help in developing skills that will assist you in speaking appropriately and effectively.

Mission advocacy may cause trustees to advocate for the independence of their school from inappropriate governmental regulations, for their students and their special needs, for independent education in general, etc. Trustees can be very effective advocates because they are not paid to do their work for the school, and, as committed volunteers, citizens, and voters, they bring credibility to their stated positions.

Trustees as Legal Fiduciaries

❖ *What do you mean I'm legally responsible for the school?*

The role of trustee as mission keeper is one of moral trusteeship. But just as moral trusteeship is a critical ingredient in maintaining a school's integrity, so are legal and financial trusteeship. Board members are individually and collectively legally liable for their actions and those of the school. Trustees are the fiduciaries of the school they govern. The board is the sole corporate identity; it alone can take action, unless such authority has been expressly delegated by the board to an individual or group of people. Individual trustees cannot commit the board or the school, unless they have been given such authority by the board, and this prohibition includes the chair, committee heads, etc.

There are four major governance areas where the board must actively exercise oversight function. They are:

◆ Corporate law, internal policies and procedures, third party contracts

◆ Local, state, and federal laws and regulations

◆ A school's financial and physical resources

◆ Risk management

Corporate Laws, Internal Policies and Procedures, Third Party Contracts

❖ *Who cares what the bylaws say?*

All trustees should understand and abide by the school's articles of incorporation or charter, and the bylaws, because these organizational documents are the internal rules for the school and the board.

◆ A school's articles of incorporation/organizational charter are filed with the appropriate state authorities and usually set forth the school's purpose, its legal authority, and any limitations to its powers. Changes need to be filed with the state.

◆ Bylaws are the procedures by which trustees govern the school, and changes or amendments must be done in accordance with procedures stated in the bylaws. Typical items in bylaws include how decisions are made, how trustees and officers are selected and elected, how the board is organized, brief officer and committee role descriptions, the governance reporting structure, especially relationship of the head to the board, etc. Bylaws should be reviewed periodically, and if amendments are proposed, they should be reviewed by the school's outside legal counsel. (Note: It is very important that a school have an independent legal counsel — see Chapter 3.)

◆ Internal institutional policies are set by the board to assure that a school's operations are conducted appropriately. The administration develops operational policies and procedures that implement broad policies and puts them into practice. Typical institutional policies are found in areas such as financial management, personnel practices, building and vehicles use, safety and risk management, protection of students, confidentiality of information, and school discipline. These institutional policies and the resulting procedures are binding, and courts of law make decisions on disputes based on what is in a school's stated policies. Do remember that a policy is not a policy unless it is written down. It also does no good if a policy is not communicated to those it concerns. (See Chapter 3 for more about policies.)

◆ Contracts between the school and third parties are binding. Boards need to have a policy that explicitly delegates the authority to sign third-party contracts to a few individuals. All trustees should know and understand what is in those contracts.

Local, State, and Federal Laws and Regulations

❖ *I thought we were independent. What's the government got to do with us?*

Every state regulates corporations, and nonprofits and educational institutions have additional statutes that apply to them. Each locality's and state's law is unique, and so it is critical for the board to be assured that the school is obeying the applicable laws and regulations. This verification can be done by reviewing reports from the head to the board and board committees, by retaining outside legal counsel, who should periodically review policies and procedures, and by hiring an insurance professional (who does not sell insurance) to review insurance coverage and risk management policies and procedures. Independent auditors can be a critical source of information on internal controls and potential business risks. Some categories of statutes are:

◆ Nonprofit corporate law

◆ Educational licensing and regulations

◆ Charitable solicitation laws (designed to protect the public from fraud and abuse)

◆ State tax exemption (Federal tax exemption status does not automatically convert to such a state status. Most states require a separate filing.)

◆ Health and Safety Codes (Designed to protect students, staff, and public.)

◆ Charitable Immunity Statutes (Most states have laws that limit the liability of nonprofits from third-party suits alleging wrongful conduct. However, few such laws have been tested in the courts.)

Schools that have an exemption from federal taxes under Section 501(c)3 of the Internal Revenue Code are also called nonprofits. Exemption from federal taxes, however, does not exempt a school from filing an IRS Form 990 each year. Also, schools must pay income withholding taxes, FICA, and any state withholding taxes for its employees.

Trustees need to assure themselves that the school is acting within:

◆ Anti-discrimination Laws. All civil rights laws apply to independent schools in their employment practices and admission to the school, including the Americans with Disabilities Act of 1990.

◆ Fair Labor Standards Act is the federal wage and hour law, including minimum wage guidelines and guidelines governing who is or is not exempt from wage and hour law.

◆ Employment Retirement Income Security Act (ERISA) regulates pension and health benefits for employees. It does not require that such benefits be offered, but if they are, they must be administered fairly.

A School's Financial and Physical Resources

❖ Why can't I just leave the finances up to the finance committee?

Often, trustees are surprised to learn that they are equally responsible for the school's financial well-being and oversight of fiscal matters. Treasurers and finance, investment (if separate from finance), buildings and grounds, and audit committees can facilitate the resource oversight role of the board, but the total board is liable when anything goes awry. It is critical, therefore, that financial reports be timely and understandable so all trustees can be fully informed. Such reports need to highlight variances to the operating budget so that board members can ask questions based on these variances. Boards do not "accept," "approve," or "adopt" financial reports, because the numbers cannot be guaranteed to be 100 percent accurate. The board should not place itself in legal jeopardy by stating that they are accurate. The yearly audited statements prepared by an independent auditor should be approved, since the auditor does testify to the accuracy of the audited figures. The board undertakes its role of financial oversight through a number of actions and committees, which bring their recommendations and reports to the board for information or action. (See Chapter 10 for more in-depth information on committees.) The following are functions that in a classic organization of the board are done by separate committees. However, a finance committee could become the resource committee, with the main committee serving as the finance committee and other subcommittees picking up the investment and physical resources functions. The audit committee should always be an independent committee.

Financial oversight

The finance committee works with staff to prepare the annual operating and capital budgets and long-range financial plan; monitors all financial activity in greater detail than the board as a whole; develops financial policies; and brings all such items to the board for its approval, along with regular financial reports for the board's information. This committee works closely with the school's business manager or chief financial officer. Frequently, the treasurer serves as chair of this committee and is the board's "point person" with the staff on financial matters. The finance committee must take care to avoid taking upon itself the setting of institutional priorities as it works through the budget.

Investment oversight

In larger schools, a separate investment committee, or a subcommittee of the finance committee, may monitor the investment of a school's endowment. Rather than manage the investments itself, this committee recommends an outside professional investment manager to the board for its approval. (Committee members generally do not have the time and/or expertise to manage school investments.) This committee interacts with the professional manager on a scheduled basis, recommends investment strategy, along with other investment policies, assures that income from gifts restricted to specific purposes is used solely for those purposes, and monitors investment performance against objectives established for the professional manager. In smaller schools, the finance committee performs this role.

Physical assets oversight

Usually the buildings and grounds committee oversees the well-being of all physical assets. The committee develops, with staff and appropriate outside consultants, a long-range master plan for space-use for board approval, and develops policies for board approval.

Independent audit

The audit committee consults with the independent auditor, recommends the annual independent audit to the board for its approval, monitors the implementation of any recommendations on internal controls contained in the auditor's management letter, and can oversee risk management activities.

Development/Fund-raising/Advancement

The development committee has general oversight of the fund-raising plans, both long range and annual. This committee, or a separate annual fund committee, implements the annual campaign, which should involve the board and other school constituencies. It may also be involved in planning and implementing special events, which can have separate committees for each event. The capital campaign committee recommends goals and purposes of the campaign for board approval, and involves first the board and then the whole school community through campaign activities and opportunities to give.

Risk Management

❖ *How could any member of this wonderful school community sue me?*

There is no way a board can establish sufficient policies and procedures in order to eliminate all risk and resulting law suits, but risk can be managed in order to keep litigation to a minimum. The board's role is to assure that the appropriate policies — such as personnel, student activities and behavior, crisis management, and financial management — are in place and that the school is following those policies and the resulting procedures every day in a consistent, fair manner. (See checklist on p. 41.)

A written conflict of interest policy, drafted by legal counsel, should set forth what constitutes a conflict, and trustees and administrators should sign a form acknowledging that they understand the policy and identifying any potential conflicts they may have. It is interesting that a major conflict of interest for most schools is parent-trustees voting on tuitions. However, they usually vote against their personal interests by raising tuitions from year-to-year. The chair should monitor any conflicts, and if a conflict should arise, the affected trustees should recuse themselves from any discussions or vote on the specific issue. Wherever appropriate, establishing a system for bids for major school purchases of goods and services is further protection against the appearance of conflicts of interest. Remember, even the appearance that trustees are enriching themselves, their families, or their businesses through service on the board, no matter if it is not the case, can damage a school's reputation.

One area that schools often overlook as part of their management of risk is that of school publications. Every school wants to present the very best picture of its program, facilities, student body, and faculty. It does this through written material, videos, electronic media (including websites), and personal contact. In all of these interactions the school and its trustees and agents must be accurate in their descriptions of current programs and practices and in their promises of what they can deliver. For example, School X promises that it offers a strong program in the arts, and then it does not invest in building a program, with well-trained faculty and dedicated facilities and materials. This discrepancy between promises and action can lead, at the very least, to a disappointed child and parents who chose the school because of the arts program. Today's independent school parents are products of the consumer age; they expect to see in action the program first described to them in the application process. It is important that trustees assure that the school promotes itself in an ethical manner, not only to avoid litigation but, above all, because it is the right thing to do.

Schools need to have directors and officers liability insurance to protect trustees from suits alleging corporate and individual wrong-doing. The policies need to cover the fees of legal counsel, as well as the monies awarded in a judgment against the school. Such policies do not cover criminal behavior or willful negligence. Therefore the best protection against a suit is an active board of trustees that exercises its governance role with great care. Ways that individual trustees can protect themselves from potential suits are found in Chapter 11.

CASE STUDY

An Unplanned Deficit

During a board meeting, the treasurer reports that there is an unplanned deficit of $75,000 in this year's budget of $5 million. No audit is planned to confirm the deficit, and the chair claims that the deficit is "not a problem, because the finance committee is on top of the situation." No one at the meeting raises any questions or objections. Since this is your first board meeting as a new trustee, you reluctantly mention to the board that you "received no copies of financial records during orientation." When you ask whether the shortfall results from a decrease in enrollment or an increase in expenses, the chair of the board tells you, "The finance committee is on top of the deficit, so you shouldn't worry about this."

What are the issues?

What should the head do?

What should the chair do?

As a new trustee, what should you do?

SAMPLE MATERIALS

RISK MANAGEMENT CHECKLIST

❐ A clear mission statement

❐ Crisis management plan

❐ Adequate insurance

    ❐ General liability

    ❐ Directors and officers liability

❐ Written policies in the areas of:

    ❐ Bloodborne pathogens

    ❐ Conflicts of interest, with forms signed by trustees and administrators acknowledging the policy and identifying potential conflicts

    ❐ Personnel — hiring, evaluation, termination

    ❐ Student code of conduct, discipline procedures

    ❐ Religious activity on campus

    ❐ Athletic safety

    ❐ Use of school bulletin boards

    ❐ Off-campus trips (and adult supervision of) — local, national, and international

    ❐ Utilization of buildings and grounds by the school community and outsiders

    ❐ Bids required for contracts for goods and services

    ❐ Financial management, especially checks and balances

    ❐ Investment management

    ❐ Admission

    ❐ Financial aid

❐ Gift acceptance

❐ A system to review policies periodically both internally and with outside professional assistance

❐ Up-to-date bylaws

❐ A strategic plan that has measurable action plans

❐ A rolling three-year financial plan

❐ Bonds for those paid staff and volunteers who handle money

❐ Publications, video, and electronic media that accurately portray the school, especially its admission policy, program, and facilities

INTERIM STATEMENT OF ACTIVITY

For the Month of April and
Ten Months Ending April 30, XXXX

	Month of April Budget	Actual	10 Months Ending April 30, XXXX Budget	Actual	(Over) Under	Year's Budget
INCOME:						
Tuition	$—	$—	$—	$—	($—)	$—
Annual Fund						
Endowment Income						
Special Events						
etc.						
TOTAL	$—	$—	$—	$—	($—)	$—
EXPENSES:						
Salaries & Benefits	$—	$—	$—	$—	—	$—
Instructional Supplies						
Faculty Development						
Trustee Development						
Maintenance						
Supplies						
etc.						
TOTAL	$—	$—	$—	$—	($—)	$—
Excess of Income over Expenses	$—	$—	$—	$—	($—)	$—
Fund balance at beginning of the period	$—	$—	$—	$—	—	$—
Fund balance at April 30, XXXX	$—	$—	$—	$—	($—)	$—

Explanations of significant variances:

A.

B.

C.

NOTE: There was an operating deficit during the month of April. This could be a sign of problems, or it could be a usual occurrence during this month. The balance for the year is still positive.

RESOURCES

Carver, John, *The CEO Role Under Policy Governance,* CarverGuide Series. Jossey-Bass, San Francisco, CA, 1996.

"Doing the Right Thing: A Look at Ethics in the Nonprofit Sector" *Board Member — Special Edition*, Volume 7 Number 5 May 1998, National Center for Nonprofit Boards.

Dorsey, Eugene C., *The Role of the Board Chairperson,* National Center for Nonprofit Boards, Washington, DC, 1992.

Leifer, Jacqueline Covey and Michael B. Glomb, *The Legal Obligations of Nonprofit Boards — A Guidebook for Board Members,* National Center for Nonprofit Boards, Washington, DC, 1997.

Zeitlin, Kim Arthur and Susan Zorn, *The Nonprofit Board's Guide to Bylaws — Creating a Framework for Effective Governance,* National Center for Nonprofit Boards, Washington, DC, 1996.

CHAPTER THREE

Developing and Reviewing Policy

If you are going to play the game properly, you'd better know every rule.

— *Barbara Jordan*

A s a trustee, you focus on broad institutional policies and leave operating policies and procedures to the school's head and administration. You make sure that board-generated policies further the school's mission and lessen risks to the school and its community through appropriate governance oversight and assessment. You are the ultimate custodian of the school's well-being, and you use your role in shaping, approving, and monitoring policies as a tool to achieve this end.

What Is Policy?

❖ *What do you mean, "It's a policy"?*

An institutional policy is a broad statement of purpose or limitation and can be developed by the board, its committees, the head, or others within the school who perceive the need for such a policy. However, the board has the authority and responsibility to approve institutional policies. Policies are implemented through procedures and rules.

Example 1:

Policy — Because the school believes in the value of a diverse teaching staff, it will recruit faculty of color. (Approved by board)

Procedure — The head of each division of the school will attend the state-wide independent school employment fair for teachers of color. (Approved by head)

Example 2:

Policy — No alcohol will be served at school events on and off campus, including to adults. (Approved by board)

Procedure — At the beginning of each school year, the Parents Association leadership will publicize the alcohol policy to all parents at its welcome-to-school meeting and in its September newsletter. (Approved by Parents Association leadership)

Policies are not policies unless they are written down, and they are not effective unless they and the resulting procedures are shared with the audience they are designed to affect — that is, the faculty, administrators, students, parents, alumnae/i, funders, vendors, outside users of facilities, or any combination of these groups.

Reasons for Policy

❖ *Why bother with policies? Don't they frustrate creativity?*

Policies are designed to be tools for boards and administrations as they:

◆ Along with the mission and strategic and operational plans, focus energies and resources,

◆ Delegate authority and still allow the board to keep control,

◆ Provide a framework in which decisions can be made and work carried out,

◆ Assure consistency of actions, especially in difficult and stressful situations, and

◆ Define the ways the school wishes to work and the board wishes to govern.

Board and Administration Roles in Shaping Policy

Isn't it confusing? Don't both boards and staff develop policies?

There is a widely held belief that the board sets policy, and the administration implements policy. The statement is true, as far as it goes. Boards do set broad institutional policies, and the administration then develops and implements procedures flowing out of the policies. However, administrators, under the leadership of the head, also develop and implement policies — broad operational policies. Trustees may be asked by the head for advice on more operational policies and should otherwise not be involved with such policies. Difficult problems arise when individual trustees interfere with the implementation of any policy, especially when students, parents, administrators, and faculty are involved. (See Chapter 9 for more information on the board's relationship with the school's many constituencies.)

Policy Development

Which policies do boards typically set? Which do heads set?

Typical board promulgated policies are:

◆ Mission statement

◆ Code of conduct/conflict of interest

◆ Bylaws

◆ Other governance policies/procedures (if not in bylaws)
　Board giving
　Board/committee meeting attendance
　Board committee participation, etc.

◆ Investment guidelines

◆ Annual budget

◆ Board self-evaluation

Typical board/head promulgated policies and procedures are:

◆ Authorization/delegation of authorization by board to head and head to staff

◆ Crisis plans

◆ Financial procedures, especially checks and balances

◆ Enrollment (linked to mission and budget)

Numbers

Type of students

◆ Employment terms

Salary ranges (head decides on individual salaries)

Benefits

Course load (faculty)

◆ Sexual harassment

◆ Buildings and grounds

◆ Use by outside groups

◆ Campus master plan

◆ Evaluation of the head by the board

◆ Policy on life-threatening illnesses — staff, students, educational efforts

Typical policies/procedures promulgated by the head and administration:

◆ Admission

Application process, including decisions on admittance

Financial aid process, including decisions on who gets what amount

◆ Administrative staffing

Staff table of organization

Job descriptions

Evaluation

◆ Faculty and staff

Academic structure

Evaluation

◆ Students

Code of conduct

Discipline procedures

Evaluation and grading system

◆ Program

Curriculum development

Extracurricular activities, including sports

◆ Systems

Administrative procedures

Information systems

No matter how carefully a board sets forth and understands the delineation of the board's role in policy development and approval, there will be occasions when confusion does occur. What trustees perceive as a board policy may be perceived by the head as an operational policy/procedure and vice-versa. Usually the solution to this disagreement is not to set more rules or guidelines, but to operate in a climate of trust and openness where differences of this type can be discussed and resolved. You, as a trustee, can play a critical role in this kind of situation by being a good listener, critical thinker, and consensus builder.

There may be times when a head will want the board's endorsement of an operational policy because the policy may be controversial — for example, the HIV/AIDS policies developed in the late 1980s. Those policies were operational in nature, dealing with students and faculty/staff as well as with curriculum content. However, HIV/AIDS was a high profile issue within the school community and with the public-at-large. Once again, nothing is as simple as it seems!

NOTE: See the "Design of the Partnership" diagram at the end of this chapter for another description of this relationship.

Procedure for forming policy

❖ *Who thought up this policy?*

The recognition that there is need for a broad institutional policy can come from a number of sources: board committees, the chair, the head, the administration and parents. Most often the head confronts a situation that should have been covered by a policy and is not. She will bring the need for a policy to the attention of the chair, and often the head will draft the policy by herself or in conjunction with the staff or with the appropriate board committee. Usually, a committee reviews the draft policy and recommends its approval by the board.

Publishing policy

❖ *I never
saw that
policy.
Where is
it written
down?*

Remember, a policy is not a policy unless it is written down. Trustees need to see and understand the policies for which they are responsible. One problem is that board generated policies are often scattered through years of board minutes and dispersed in various committee files and school offices. Although policies are in effect until they are officially repealed, many trustees are surprised to find that some policies are still technically on the books, though not followed. For example, ten years ago a policy stated in the board minutes that trustees need not attend meetings and now they are expected to do so, but the policy was never repealed. Trustees, therefore, need to either have a policy notebook, with all of the board generated policies in it, or a list of policies and where they can be found.

On the other hand, the faculty/administration and student handbooks should be shared with trustees for information purposes only.

Now that you have navigated the turbulent waters of policy formulation, approval, and monitoring, you may wish to take a deep breath and then review a few of the policies the board has approved. Are they truly broad institutional policies? Who has played a role in shaping them? When were they set? What procedures have been developed to implement them? Then look at the list of board policies to see if any are missing. If no such list exists, suggest that such a list, if not a policy manual, be developed.

As a trustee, you are the keeper of the mission, and so you need to be sure that the policies are in concert with the mission. As a trustee, you are the fiduciary for the school, and so you need to be sure that policies are in place that prevent wrongdoing. In fact, policies can further all aspects of your trusteeship role; they are major governance tools.

Policies and accreditation

When your school prepares its self-study for an accreditation, you will find the governance standards frequently look for evidence of policies in many areas noted above.

Legal Concerns

We need a lawyer. Can we use a board member?

Years ago many schools elected, often by default, to have the school's lawyer be any one of a series of attorneys who happened to be members of the board. This is not a procedure NAIS recommends, for inevitably the attorney is faced with a major conflict of interest, particularly when it comes to resolving difficult cases where the board itself may be the subject of litigation, real or threatened. And, alas, many frivolous lawsuits are now taking the time — and dollars — of independent schools today.

Small schools with limited resources may still fall into this practice, but as a basic guideline, NAIS strongly urges schools, in addition to whatever legal advisors they may have on their board, to consider hiring an external lawyer on retainer. The attorney does not need to be an expert in school law. In fact, the generalist position can help, as most school law is public school law. Areas of legal expertise many independent schools have found useful include: contract law, employment law, disabilities law, and sexual harassment.

Budgeting for legal counsel

How can a school plan to budget and pay for such advice, especially a school with a tight budget?

One school we know has an agreement with its counsel, who bills them at a reduced percentage of the firm's normal rate (the other part is considered pro bono), to accrue all bills incurred in one fiscal year for payment in the next. That way, if a school has an unusually high need to consult the attorney — and that can happen, unplanned situations emerge, creating a need for unplanned expense — the bills can be budgeted for in the subsequent fiscal year. That way, a head, board chair, or business officer is never watching the meter, debating whether or not to call the lawyer.

When in doubt, call your lawyer, and we hope that lawyer is *not* a member of your board.

CASE STUDY

Social Promotion and Big Money

(Individual Trustees and Academic Standards)

Smart Stuff Academy has long had a commitment to excellence in education and promotes the school as a place for the academically serious. Johnny, the son of the school's most generous benefactors, is about to fail the third grade (again). His teachers indicate that Johnny is highly intelligent but chooses not to do his lessons. One senior board member takes up Johnny's cause, arguing that the board should require Johnny be passed on to the fourth grade, both for social reasons and because his father has linked his next significant dollar gift to his only son's progress through his alma mater. Several board members (and all of Johnny's teachers) balk at the pressure exerted on the board by Johnny's father, claiming that the school's academic standards would be forever compromised if the board caved in to his demand.

What are the issues?

What should the board do?

What should the head do?

What should the chair do?

SAMPLE MATERIALS

DESIGN OF THE PARTNERSHIP

Policies	Time and Attention Graph
Strategies mission survival leadership major	**Board's Decisions** Head's Advice
Partnership authorizations finance policies enrollment employment terms	**Shared Decisions: Board and Head**
Operational admissions staffing program systems	Board's Advice **Head's Decisions**

Above the diagonal line = allocation of board's time
Below the diagonal line = allocation of head's time

Board Policy Checklist

Boards will vary in the written policies they adopt, but the following list serves as a useful point of departure for consideration.

Hint: it is helpful always to print in **bold** or CAPITAL LETTERS statements of board policies in minutes of board meetings. Then they are easily traceable. New trustee orientation should include either copies of the relevant minutes, or a separate policy statement document, with dates passed, reaffirmed etc.

Topics for board policy:

- ❒ clear mission statement
- ❒ crisis management plan

- ❒ adequate insurance
  general liability
  directors and officers

Written policies in the areas of:

- ❒ conflict of interest, with forms signed annually by trustees and administrators, acknowledging the policies and potential conflicts

- ❒ personnel/hiring/evaluation/ termination

- ❒ student code of conduct/ discipline procedures/due process

- ❒ final say in dismissal of students or employees (rests with the head)

- ❒ utilization of buildings and grounds by school community and outsiders

- ❒ bids required for contract goods and services

- ❒ financial management, especially checks and balances

- ❒ investment management, spending rate, etc.

- ❒ admission/preferences (if any) and other policies

- ❒ financial aid

- ❒ gifts acceptance policies/naming policies

- ❒ a system to review policies periodically, both internally and externally with outside professional assistance

- ❒ up-to-date bylaws

- ❒ a strategic plan that has measurable action plans

- ❒ a rolling three-year financial plan

- ❒ bonds for paid staff and volunteers who handle money

- ❒ publications, video, and electronic media that accurately portray the school, especially the admission policies and the facilities

RESOURCES

Carver, John and Miriam Mayhew Carver, *Reinventing Your Board*, Jossey-Bass, San Francisco, CA, 1997.

Chait, Richard P., *How to Help Your Board Govern More and Manage Less*, National Center for Nonprofit Boards, Washington, DC, 1993.

Taylor, Barbara E., Richard P. Chait, and Thomas P. Holland, *"The New Work of the Board,"* Harvard Business Review, September-October 1996.

CHAPTER FOUR

Developing a Shared Vision and Planning Strategically

The first responsibility of a leader is to define reality.

— Max Dupree

We invite you to dream about the things that can really make a difference in the lives of students and faculty.

— Walter Burgin

As a trustee, you are the mission's trustholder, you serve as a legal fiduciary of the school's well-being, and participate in the formation, approval, and monitoring of broad institutional policies. One of the tools you need to be able to undertake your many roles is a strategic plan that is derived from the mission of and vision for the school. You may or may not participate directly in the planning process, but you will, as a member of the board, approve an amended mission statement or affirm the current one. You may also approve a vision statement, which not every planning process develops, and will approve the goals of the plan. In short, you plan for the future of the school for which you care.

The bridge between the school's mission and its policies is a strategic plan. Such a plan will set forth what a school must accomplish in the next three-to-five years in order to thrive, as it strives to fulfill its mission in the most effective manner possible. The plan takes into account the external and internal world in which a school exists, establishes goals and action plans that guide yearly operational plans, and sets forth methods and timetables for evaluation, which facilitates corrections to the plan, if necessary. (See p.68 for the definitions of planning terms. You do not need to agree with the terms, but it is important for you to understand how the terms are used in this chapter in order for the process to make sense to you.)

The Need to Plan

❖ *Why should anyone spend valuable time on planning when there is so much else to do?*

Trustees need to be convinced that strategic planning will be beneficial for the school as a whole and for the board in its governance role. The following are just some of the reasons to plan. A school can:

Control its future

A school cannot control all of the external forces with which it interacts, but it must not drift along, buffeted by whatever force or individual is strongest at the moment.

◆ The school can consider options and choose the best path for the school at a moment in its history.

◆ It can plan for contingencies.

◆ It can be more flexible and adaptable.

◆ The school can have greater assurance that it will remain truly independent and true to its own mission.

Maximize resources

Resources, human and financial, are tight for almost every school. Planning can assist in establishing priorities for resource allocations in order to best meet the school's needs and fulfill its mission.

Develop and sustain a shared sense of direction

As the various school constituencies work together assessing the school's current status and planning for the future, they develop a shared sense of direction. This synergy can increase the probability of the plan's success.

Prepare for a capital campaign

Strategic planning should be the precursor of a capital campaign. Such a plan establishes the "why" of a campaign, which underlies the case statement of the campaign, and allows the board to set priorities among a multitude of funding needs.

Inspire motivation for accomplishing the plan's activities

If the planning process includes all school constituencies, it can be a vehicle that motivates people to accomplish the established goals. Those involved in the planning process ultimately feel a sense of ownership of the plan and want it to succeed.

Instill quality

A strategic plan can be marked by the critical importance of quality in all that it does and by establishing ongoing procedures that evaluate the level of quality.

Improve public relations

A good process and the resulting plan can help a school's constituencies articulate where the school is going and why. Establishing clarity of mission and delineating measurable results allows everyone to tell the school's story internally and externally.

Who Should Be in the Planning Process?

❖ *Why can't a few trustees go away for the weekend and come back with a plan for the school?*

A critical component of any planning process is the constitution of the planning committee/task force. The quality, the breadth and depth of the plan, the ability to move the plan forward and generate enthusiasm throughout the school community, all depend on who is involved in the process. A core group — whose members come from every part of the school community — should facilitate the process. All trustees, along with the board chair and the school head, need to be involved. Faculty, administrators, parents, and alumnae/i also need to be involved. One individual can wear several "hats," but no one should represent a single constituency. Rather, everyone should bring his or her experiences to the planning deliberations and yet plan for the school as a whole.

In order to undertake an effective planning process it is not mandatory that a school hire an outside consultant, but an outside consultant can be very helpful in keeping track of the process and allowing all involved to participate equally. Consultant fees vary greatly and depend on the scope of work for which the school contracts. It is important to engage a consultant who does not come to a school with a rigid prepackaged process or preconceived outcomes.

Others in the school, beyond the core planning group, can be involved in the process during various phases, such as the stages of information gathering, brainstorming possibilities, etc. The more inclusive the process, the wider the acceptance of the finished product — the plan. This inclusivity needs to be balanced with the importance of accomplishing the process in a timely and cost effective manner.

Basic Planning Process

❖ *Where are we in the process — step 7 or 23?*

Planning processes can be very complicated with a multitude of steps. However, a simple process is easier to manage and explain. No matter how many stages there are in the process, there are seven basic ones.

1. Planning to plan

◆ Get the board and administration to support the need for and budget for a strategic plan and recognize the benefits to the school of such a plan.

◆ Select the planning committee/task force and its leadership.

◆ Decide whether or not to hire an outside consultant, and, if the answer is yes, select and hire the consultant.

◆ Establish the planning process and its timelines.

2. Gather information about and assess the environment

This step can consume a great amount of time and be very costly. The planning committee/task force can never know everything about everything, so it must set priorities. Which information is critical? How should the board elicit such information in order to develop the best plan for the school?

◆ External Information Gathering — What are the opportunities and threats in the school's environment? What's going on out there?

Examples of methods:

◆ Conduct surveys, interviews, and focus groups of various external groups about the major issues facing the community, public and independent institutions, and higher education.

◆ Do the same with internal groups about the their perceptions of the external world.

◆ Collect census data for demographics.

◆ Collect data from NAIS and state/regional associations.

◆ Internal information gathering: What are the school's strengths and weaknesses? How are we doing?

Examples of methods:

◆ Conduct surveys, interviews, and focus groups of both internal constituents and outsiders about their perceptions of the school. They could include:

Students

Parents

Faculty

Administrators

Alumnae/i

Administrators, teachers, or other representatives from colleges your students go on to attend

Community leaders

Funders

◆ If it exists, review progress toward the previous strategic plan.

◆ Collect information on internal trends, such as enrollment, tuition, fund-raising, financial aid, etc.

◆ Collect comparative data about other schools you choose to use as benchmarks and gather information from state/regional associations.

3. Develop the strategic plan's mission, vision, and goals

Planning committees/task forces have found that retreats of at least a day can be very helpful at the beginning and end of the planning process. They can:

◆ Generate strategic issues and set priorities of importance.

◆ Develop goals that address the major critical issues. (The tendency is to establish too many goals. The fewer the better — say five to seven.)

◆ Establish the school's mission and the statement that describes the mission, or, if the mission and its statement already exist, examine them very critically. To affirm the mission and its statement intentionally is just as valid as altering them.

◆ Develop a vision of the school at least ten years in the future and a statement that vividly describes that vision. (Not all planning processes involve this step, but establishing and communicating a vision can be very energizing and unifying for the school.)

◆ Check the goals to affirm that they further the mission and lead to the attainment of the vision.

◆ Draft the written strategic plan, which should include:

Description of the planning process,

Vision statement (if part of the process),

Mission statement,

Broad institutional goals, with accompanying rationales and underlying strategic priorities, and

Explanation of next steps.

NOTE: *This process ends with the mission and vision. Many begin with them. Whichever method is chosen, the mission is the key component of the planning process and its successful implementation.*

4. Develop action plans and more detailed yearly operational plans

These set forth how each goal will be met. Please note that action plans can consist of objectives and strategies or lists of activities. The staff, under the leadership of the head, shoulders most of the responsibility for the development and implementation of such plans. Boards and their committees may establish their own yearly operational plans to focus the board on its own work to further the strategic plan.

◆ Establish responsibilities and the resulting accountability of individuals, committees, task forces, academic and administrative departments, etc.

◆ Set timelines, remembering that you have more than one year to accomplish the plan.

◆ Monitor and evaluate the plan's progress at pre-established intervals.

5. Approval of the plan

Official approval is done by the board of trustees, which is ultimately responsible for the accomplishment of the plan. Please note that the board approves the mission and vision statements and the organizational strategic goals. Unless the action plans involve the work of the board or major cost for their implementation, the board does not vote on these operational plans. In some planning processes, the action steps are only developed after the board has approved the goals.

◆ Keep every trustee informed of the planning process all during the development of the plan.

◆ Include board committees in the planning process, where appropriate, such as assisting in information gathering and brainstorming critical issues within the committee's area of responsibility.

◆ Send the plan out ahead to the board and allow sufficient time for the board to deliberate at either a board meeting dedicated solely to the plan or at a retreat for that same purpose.

6. Celebrate and communicate the plan (mission, vision, and goals) to all school constituencies

◆ Use newsletters, meetings, or a special mailing which outlines the process and who was involved, and sets forth the mission, vision, and goals, with their rationales.

◆ As the plan unfolds, communicate accomplishments at meetings of the board, staff, faculty, parents, students, alumnae/i, and others. This will keep the plan alive and off the shelf!

7. Implement the plan

This is the most difficult and important part of the planning process. Will Rogers said, "Even if you're on the right track, you must keep moving or you'll get run over."

Evaluate the total plan at least once a year

❖ *What have we done?*

Evaluation is a board responsibility, and initially should include all those involved in the development of the plan. Please note that individual components of the plan may require more frequent monitoring by board committees or the total board, and the original plan should contain the schedule for these evaluations. Some boards use key indicators of success, where certain activities or goals that are critical to the accomplishment of the plan are highlighted at predetermined intervals. An example of another method of measuring strategic indicators follows.

◆ Assess the status of each goal and its strategic issues.

◆ Make corrections when necessary. The plan should never be viewed as cast in concrete. Circumstances change and the plan should be adjusted where appropriate.

Strategic Indicators for Independent Schools

Strategic planning and equally strategic execution are the hallmarks of a well-run business or school. In an era when independent schools are seeing their governing boards include many people for whom nonprofit trusteeship is a new experience — indeed, for whom independent schools themselves are a new experience — it is all too easy for some boards to focus on issues on the near horizon and become overly involved with the current school year.

The real job of trusteeship is to plan for and assure the school of tomorrow, and that important task involves taking some regular measures of where the school has been, where it is today, and where it wants and is able to go next.

A recent study, *Strategic Indicators for Higher Education*,* offers one hundred indicators used as benchmarks by over a thousand public and private

---

* *Strategic Indicators for Higher Education: Vital Benchmarks and Information to Help You Evaluate and Improve Your School's Performance.* Barbara E. Taylor and William F. Massy, Peterson's, 1997.

colleges and universities. While not all the indicators apply equally to independent schools, there are clear lessons for us in this study. Let's look at their "Big Ten Indicators" adjusted for independent schools.

1. Revenue Structure What are the sources of your school's revenue stream? Have you become more or less tuition dependent? How stable and reliable have the patterns of income been in the last five years? What changes can you reasonably anticipate? What are the trends in your non-tuition sources? Some scholars suggest the value of quasi-endowment is one of an institution's strongest signs of health. Unlike restricted gifts to endowment (for financial aid, faculty salaries, etc.), board-designated surpluses (or quasi-endowment) reflect the capacity of the school to apply present savings toward future needs.

2. Expenditure Structure What are the principal uses of and trends in expenditure? What changes are likely in the future? Many colleges, seeing financial aid grow rapidly in the past ten years, are scaling back on these dollars as a percentage of overall expenditures. Some member schools have reluctantly, but responsibly, come to similar conclusions.

3. Budget Excess/Deficit What is the difference between current revenue and expenses? How long could you operate without additional sources of income? If you have incurred deficits, how have they been dealt with? Over-reliance on one or two sources to cover deficits is a dangerous practice and can jeopardize long-term financial stability.

4. Enrollment Data What is the percentage of applicants accepted at key entry points? What percent of those accepted enroll? Examine student attrition patterns. How, and how readily, are departing students replaced?

5. Student/Faculty Ratio This statistic — oft-quoted by independent schools to reflect individual attention and small class size — is also a measure of workload and productivity. How does it look when broken out by division or grade levels, by subject, and by teacher?

6. Financial Aid As requests for financial aid from low and middle income families grow, schools should measure the annual picture in two ways: 1) aid as a percentage of total tuition and fee income, and 2) net tuition income (total tuition charged minus aid awarded). Changes over time merit thoughtful analysis.

7. Faculty Profile Schools need to keep an eye on their overall faculty profile. What is the percentage of beginning teachers? Those with five-ten years experience, ten-fifteen years, fifteen-twenty years, over twenty years in the classroom? Funding and achieving educational goals will be affected by factors identified in such a profile. It is also informative to determine whether the full-time faculty as a percentage of all staff is increasing, decreasing, or holding steady.

8. Demographics
What are the diversity indicators at your school? What are your marketplace factors, goals, and actual achievements in recruitment, retention, and advancement of students and staff of color? Have you examined staff gender balance and related compensation issues? What is the demographic profile of your financial aid students: grade levels, income, gender, ethnicity, geographic distribution?

9. Deferred Maintenance
What is your estimated maintenance backlog (even if imprecise) as a percentage of total plant replacement value? Schools that have chosen to focus on other priorities in recent years (financial aid, faculty salaries, technology) can find this a disturbing figure.

10. Giving Trends What percentage of your alumni/ae have contributed to the school in the last five years? What percentage of parents? Try to imagine how a foundation or corporation would view such a show of support. Trustees must set the tone with 100 percent participation.

In many of these areas, schools will want to ask a corollary question: How do our data compare with those from our peer institutions? Data vary by region, school, and grade range. While each institution must establish its own goals, a comparison of strategic indicators with peer schools helps inform institutional priorities. For trustees working in NAIS member schools, it is helpful to know that NAIS does offer comparative data in a variety of areas (contact NAIS's statistics office at 202-973-9700).

If your school is not presently taking its own measure in these ways, try using the above questions as the basis of an exercise at your next board meeting. Without collecting or grading their quiz papers, ask each trustee to answer these questions. The exercise should help move the group toward understanding how to best use the time and talents of its members as guardians of the future of your institution.

Prepare to plan — again!

❖ *Are we doing this again?*

Once a strategic plan has been established, some boards add an extra year to the plan, as part of its yearly assessment. This results in what is called a "rolling plan." Even with these yearly plan additions, the best boards do undertake a full planning process at least every five years. Other boards begin a formal planning process in the last year of the current plan.

With the strategic planning process, it is not only appropriate to go around in a circle, it is mandatory.

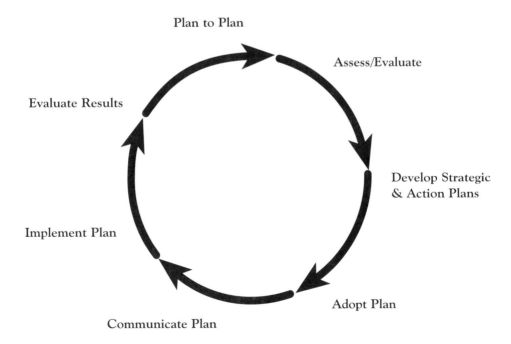

Plan to Plan

Assess/Evaluate

Develop Strategic & Action Plans

Adopt Plan

Communicate Plan

Implement Plan

Evaluate Results

As a trustee, you may be an active participant in the total planning process or in a section of it. You will, as a member of the board, examine the proposed plan carefully to be sure that it contains a mission and vision that reflect the school's beliefs and desired program not only in the present but also in the future. You will also make sure that the goals will enable the school to fulfill its mission and achieve its vision and that they are viable. You want the school and all who serve it to reach for excellence so that its students will be productive and caring citizens who comport their lives with integrity.

Definitions of Planning Terms

There are almost as many planning processes as there are consultants. To say that this can lead to confusion is an understatement. The following term definitions can be your guide. It's important that when you and your school enter into a planning process that everyone involved agrees on the terminology.

Note: Not all boards require all of the following terms as steps in their planning process. For instance, some boards don't create both objectives and strategies. Others see no need for a vision statement or a philosophy statement. But a planning scenario must include, at a minimum, a mission statement, goals, and strategies.

The **Mission Statement** of a school describes why the school exists:

◆ what the school believes

◆ who it serves

◆ what it does

The statement should be succinct and a guide to the actions of the board, administration, and faculty. A mission statement that truly captures the essence of a school inspires energy and commitment.

The **Vision Statement** (optional for schools) describes the school's desired future. It is an image of an ideal, an expression of optimism.

A **Philosophy Statement** (also optional for schools) expresses a school's bedrock values and beliefs about its educational program, students, faculty, support services, sense of community, etc. It often supports and augments the mission statement.

A **Goal** is a broad institutional statement of intent. Sometimes such goals are called "policy goals."

Example: The school will increase its non-tuition income.

An **Objective** describes how a goal will be achieved. It is concrete and measurable and can be assigned to a specific individual or group for implementation and accountability.

Example: The annual fund campaign will increase by 5 percent each of the next three years.

A **Strategy** is even more specific than an objective and often is called an "action step."

Example: The development committee will add a grandparent component to the annual campaign within the next three months.
Note: Usually there are more detailed steps under each of these action steps or strategies.

Action Plans can consist of objectives and strategies or just lists of action steps.

Yearly Operational Plans are one-year action plans that are derived from the strategic plan and from plans that keep the school going on a daily basis. The school's administration, under the leadership of the head, develops, implements, and monitors the operational plan. The board is informed of the status of the operating plan items that affect the accomplishment of the strategic plan and any other activities that might rise to the level of the board because of a crisis, unanticipated major cost factors, etc. Boards can adopt their own operating plans in order to bring focus to their work and to facilitate the assessment of their work

The **Annual Budget** is based on the Yearly Operational Plan.

CASE STUDY

What's the Plan?

Parents of students at Generation X Academy have become increasingly alarmed at the rift between the school head and its board. The head wants to steer the academy toward a closer alliance with local industry in an effort to gain corporate funding for large projects, while the board believes that establishing and maintaining a top-notch athletic program will bring far more revenue and prestige to the school. Shouting matches develop in meetings between the head and the board. The academy begins to founder. Industry wants no part of a school in such turmoil, and elite coaches and athletes want clear evidence of a strong institutional commitment to athletics before they sign on at the academy.

What are the issues?

What should the board do?

What should the head do?

What should the chair do?

SAMPLE MATERIALS

Action Plan Form

Goals:

Action	Responsibility	Target Date	Resources Needed	Approval Authority	How and By When?

RESOURCES

Evans, Robert, *The Human Side of School Change*, Jossey-Bass, San Francisco, CA, 1996.

Howe, Fisher, *The Board Member's Guide to Strategic Planning — A Practical Approach to Strengthening Nonprofit Organizations,* Jossey-Bass, San Francisco, CA, 1997.

Rouse, William B., *Don't Jump to Solutions — Thirteen Delusions that Undermine Strategic Thinking,* Jossey-Bass, San Francisco, CA, 1997.

Stone, Susan C., *Shaping Strategy — Independent School Planning in the '90s,* National Association of Independent Schools, Washington, DC, 1993.

CHAPTER FIVE

Assuring the Financial Strength of the School/Fund-Raising

I am just beginning to learn about philanthropy.

— *Bill Gates*

The school's mission is your guide in all of your actions, whether it be in planning for the future or developing policy. You are a steward of the school's resources — its people, its buildings and grounds, and its funds. One of the ways you exercise your stewardship is to assure that the school has a secure, diversified funding base. As a school leader, you are among the first to contribute your personal financial resources. You are a trustholder of all that is the school, including its funds, and a model of giving for all to emulate.

Please note that this chapter is not meant to be a primer on independent school fund-raising. For more information on fund-raising, read NAIS's book, *Philanthropy at Independent Schools*, by Helen A. Colson — the best resource on independent school giving.

The Need to Raise Funds

❖ *Why do we have to raise all this money?*

Schools do not raise funds just for the fun of it; they do it to fulfill their missions and visions. Tuition at most schools does not cover the cost of educating students and the cost of providing all of the other services expected of independent schools today. Some schools depend heavily on tuition, especially K-8 day schools. Such reliance on tuitions means that full enrollment is critical to assuring that a school can carry out its program. The danger of relying so heavily on tuition is that decisions may be made to further the growth of the student body that can compromise the school's mission, its ability to serve all its students, and thus its integrity. It would be better if a school had diversified funding sources: annual campaign dollars, endowment income, special event income, grants, bequests and other planned gifts, and in-kind donations of goods and services. Think of a one-legged stool and one with seven legs. Which one of these stools would give you the most secure seat?

❖ *I give my time. You want my money also?*

Yes. If the board of trustees wishes the school's funding base to be secure and strong, each trustee must play a role. The primary rule of fund-raising states that you cannot ask for a contribution until you make one yourself. Why should anyone give to the school if the leadership does not give? Trustees need to make significant gifts, according to their abilities to do so, and make them at the beginning of the campaign. (If a board member wishes to make a pledge, that is fine. However, they need to fulfill that pledge by the deadline.) The current standard of board participation is 100 percent, and, increasingly, foundations and individuals will give only if it can be demonstrated that all of the trustees have given or pledged. The primary trustee role in fund development is to give.

Perceived Barriers to Involvement in Development/Fund-Raising

❖ *I'll do anything except raise funds.*

Trustees often offer a number of reasons for their reluctance to ask others for money. Among them are:

◆ *"I don't know how."*

Offer training and a "buddy" system where trustees go in pairs (one experienced and one a neophyte) to ask for a gift.

◆ *"It's the responsibility of the head and director of development."*

Go back and reorient board members to their responsibilities, and be sure that the committee on trustees tells prospective trustees that they are expect-

74

ed to give and to ask for money. No one should be appointed to the board until he or she understands and heartily accepts this role.

◆ *"I'll be asked to give a gift in return."*

"Asks" should be for the school, not as a favor to the person making the request. However, this "tit for tat" mentality does exist, and trustees need to think how they might turn such a response back to the commitment they share for the school.

◆ *"I don't know anyone with money."*

This often is not true, but if a trustee believes it to be so, a director of development and fund development committee chair can work with the trustee to examine his/her connections. Perhaps the trustee could generate a list of potential donors from reviewing an address book, parents of children in his/her child's class, etc. In this case, the board member might not be asked to make the contact, but she/he will have participated in the fund development process and may be motivated to move into other activities over time.

◆ *"I did it once, and it was a disaster."*

Have the trustee make thank-you calls to donors without asking for a gift or cajole them into going with a seasoned solicitor to a donor who is sure to make a gift. The latter will give them a taste of success.

◆ *"I just don't have the time."*

Trustees need to see fund-raising as a priority. Even with little time available, a trustee can make one call per semester, especially if the development office is well-staffed. If the call can further other interests of the trustee, he/she may agree to do more calls.

◆ *"I don't understand why the school needs all this money."*

Education of the trustee is key here. However, if the trustee does not understand the case for fund-raising, she/he may be so disconnected from the school and the board that a more fundamental conversation with the board member may be necessary. It could also be the case that the total board has not discussed the school's critical issues, including the need for funds, and the board's role in their solutions — including raising monies.

Role of Trustees in Development

Trustees can contribute to fund development through a variety of activities. After making their personal gift, they can offer an opportunity to others to support the school by contributing financial resources. In fact, board members usually assume leadership positions in fund-raising activities by chairing the development committee and other committees that garner funds, such as the annual fund, special events, planned giving, and the capital campaign. All trustees should participate in development efforts according to their skills, contacts, and experience. The chief cheerleader of the board's role in fund-raising must be the chair of the board. If the chair does not embrace this role, it will be very difficult to enlist other trustees. Even though there are times when a head may wish he/she had a "fund-raising board," such a wish may lead to more money but also to a lack of understanding of the mission.

A head should really desire a "board that raises funds."

There are a number of specific fund development activities in which trustees can be involved, as the school seeks major gifts.

◆ Assessment — help the development officer or fund-raising leadership "rate" capacity to give based on knowledge of the prospect.

◆ Identify and assist in the cultivation of donors, even if they do not ask for the gift. This effort could include speaking formally or informally to parents, past parents, alumnae/i, and friends of the school and hosting events at which the head can speak about the school. The latter can be especially helpful for gatherings of alumnae/i, parents, and past parents in locations outside the school's geographic region.

◆ "Open the door" for solicitations. A trustee can schedule the meeting for others to attend or can accompany others to the meeting. The likelihood of success at such meetings is increased when trustees make the initial contact and attend the meeting, along with the head or the director of development or another trustee.

◆ Make sure that the case for the "ask" is compelling and matches the donor's interests. If the interest is unknown, time needs to be spent to learn more about the donor. In some cases, it may take several visits before you ask for a gift and even a few more before you receive the contribution.

◆ Ask for a donation. Trustees, or other volunteers, are the most appropriate people to actually request the gift. The head, director of development, and other school employees can be perceived by donors as having a conflict of interest because the funds could go toward supporting their salaries. Trustees and other volunteers are seen as making such requests simply because they care for the school.

◆ Personally thank donors and stay in touch with them. Good stewardship of the relationship between the donor and the school greatly facilitates the next request. Do keep donors informed on how their gifts have supported the work of the school.

Reaching your fund-raising goals

❖ *How does the board assure that the school will raise what it needs?*

Beyond "giving and getting" there are other board fund development responsibilities. They must:

◆ Budget sufficient funds to cover the cost of fund-raising activities, which, today, most often include the salaries of a director of development and additional staff, if that is possible. Directors of development are among the more highly compensated school personnel. Never expect to pay a director a low salary and then give them a percentage of funds raised. This behavior is considered unethical by all of the fund-raising professional associations and monitoring organizations.

◆ Develop with the staff an annual development plan, which takes into account current and future operational and capital needs and is in concert with the goals of the strategic plan.

◆ Monitor the fund development efforts to assure that they are well managed in a cost-effective manner and that the funds are used as promised to donors.

◆ When fund-raising goals are set as part of the budget, be satisfied that they are realistic, and not just a "plug" number to balance the budget.

Types of Development Activities

❖ I never knew there were so many ways people can give.

Even though this chapter is not meant to be Fund-Raising 101, trustees need to be aware of all the various ways a school can raise money. This is not only important for their general knowledge, it may also awaken an interest in working on one of the activities or contributing funds in a different way than they traditionally have or augmenting their current giving. These ways include annual fund development, capital campaigns, endowment campaigns, and planned giving (deferred gifts).

Annual fund — This fund includes personal solicitations and mail appeals. There usually are different levels of giving, with the greatest amount of attention going to major donors.

Grants — Foundations, especially family foundations, are an increasing source of funds for independent schools, both for operating funds and special projects. Corporate foundations are less likely to give grants, unless they match their employees' gifts to schools.

Special Events — These take significant time and effort on the part of volunteers and staff, but the right event can produce important dollars and reach people beyond the school community. They can be excellent opportunities to raise the school's visibility and bring new friends into the fold. However, make sure that the events are truly efficient and meet their established goals. Many schools have a number of special events during the year, but if there are too many, staff and volunteers will burn out. Worse, they will think they "have already given." Be critical in your assessment of every event; some raise so little money that the return may be in cents-per-volunteer hour. Remember, that the most cost-effective way to raise the most money is to directly ask individuals for contributions.

Capital campaigns — These campaigns raise substantial amounts of funds in order to finance buildings or property improvements. The campaigns can include construction or purchase of buildings, purchase of land, renovations, or purchase of new equipment.

Endowment campaigns — These are designed to raise major funds to increase the school's endowment. The income from the endowment can relieve the operating budget and is often restricted by donors to specific areas, such as faculty salaries, financial aid, maintenance of buildings and grounds, and special projects.

Some campaigns combine capital and endowment goals. These major fund development efforts should only be undertaken after a feasibility study has been done by an outside consultant in order to learn if a school should commit to a campaign, where support will come from, and what the goal should be. It is the board's role to establish a campaign — its purposes and financial goal.

Planned giving (deferred gifts) — These are gifts to schools from individuals, primarily through bequests, charitable remainder trusts, pooled income funds, gift annuities, and life insurance policies. This is an area in which colleges and universities have excelled for many years. It takes expertise to bring these gifts to the school, but over time the effort can pay great dividends to the funding of the school. Trustees can lead by example by working with the school to develop their own planned gifts and encouraging others to do so.

As a trustee, you contribute to the attainment of the goal of 100 percent board member participation in school funding campaigns, as well as a planned gift, if appropriate. Only you can decide what is the right amount to give, according to your capacity, but you make the school one of your top charitable contributions. You are a giver of time, talents, and treasure.

Elementary Schools and Fund-Raising

Elementary schools may find a fund development program very problematical, but they need to establish such a program no matter what the difficulties may be. The graduates of schools that range from pre-K–8 go on to high schools, then to college and universities, and often to graduate schools. Each of these institutions has a claim on the graduate's loyalty and funds, and they may stand between the elementary school and its graduates. Pre-K–8 schools may not have cultivated their graduates, but they should undertake a program that reconnects graduates to their first school or strengthens current connections. Young parents may find it more difficult to give major gifts during their children's first school years, but they should be encouraged to begin the habit of giving as early as is possible and be thanked generously for whatever contributions they make. Elementary schools can make a compelling case for funding, and they deserve their piece of the independent school funding pie. Some schools have found that a goal of 100 percent parent support, regardless of the size of the gift, is a good community builder. Of course, as is true in all schools, solicitation of major prospects generates the most funds.

CASE STUDY

Fund-Raising Auction

An urban school, whose hallmark is a long-standing commitment to diversity, uses an annual auction as its primary fund-raiser. Last year, the auction generated over $75,000 in funds to supplement the annual operating budget. This year, the school's 50th anniversary, promises even greater revenues. The event normally brings bidding from beyond the school community, but the committee wants to provide more community outreach than in past years. The committee proposes to move the auction from the school's gymnasium to an elite country club, which is widely known to have restrictive membership policies. The chair of the board notes that a board-adopted policy prevents the school from holding events in venues whose membership policies are discriminatory. The event chair, a major donor to the school, believes that since this is a special year for the school, the school should hold the event off-site. "This particular location will increase our visibility in the community," he insists, "and bring in a substantial number of wealthy prospective donors to the event, expanding our fund-raising potential."

What are the issues?

What should the chair do?

What should the head do?

SAMPLE MATERIALS

Development (Fund Development, Fund-Raising, Resource Development) Committee

Job Description

Responsibilities

The primary role of the development committee shall be to advise the board and staff of the school on all matters pertaining to fund development and to oversee and coordinate the ongoing fund development efforts of the school.

The specific committee responsibilities of the committee shall be to:

◆ Establish fund development goals and organizational structures.

◆ Approve the annual fund development plan (including the case statement, calendar, budget, goals, etc.) and inform the board. The board would approve the goal as part of the annual budget process.

◆ Identify ways trustees can be involved in the raising of funds and match individual board members with the activities that match his or her skills and interests.

◆ Identify and assist with the recruitment of the volunteers (including parents and alumnae/i) for the various activities.

◆ Assist in the identification of major donors.

◆ Make contacts with and/or "asks" with major donors, where a committee member is the right person to make such a contact.

◆ Advise on the community relations and communications plan as it relates to fund development activities for the year.

◆ Monitor the progress of the annual campaign and keep board informed.

◆ Coordinate with the capital campaign committee, if the school is undertaking such a campaign.

◆ Establish and implement a system of recognition for board and other volunteers who are active in fund-raising.

Committee Members and Staff

Development committee members should be people who:

◆ Are committed givers to the school

◆ Believe in the mission of the school

◆ Are skilled in fund-raising or willing to learn the skills to do the job

◆ Highly regarded by the school community

◆ Willing to give the necessary time

◆ The size of the committee depends on the amount of tasks to be accomplished, but not so large that the chair spends all his/her time facilitating meetings and other logistics. Seven to ten members is the average.

◆ The committee should be staffed by the development director or the head or her/his designee, if there is no development director.

Meetings

◆ The development committee should meet at least quarterly. There are times, however, when the committee may need to increase the regular frequency of these meetings to monthly or even weekly. In addition, members should also be on call for individual assignments. Development committees in boarding schools especially may need to utilize technology for their meetings, since quarterly or more meetings may be difficult.

RESOURCES

Aitken, H. Peter, *Access and Affordability: Strategic Planning Perspectives for Independent Schools*, National Association of Independent Schools, Washington, DC, 1994.

The Chronicle of Philanthropy, Washington, DC (periodical).

Colson, Helen A., *Philanthropy at Independent Schools*, National Association of Independent Schools, Washington, DC, 1996.

Foundation News, Council on Foundations, Washington, DC (periodical).

Johnson, Sandra L., *The Audit Committee,* National Center for Nonprofit Boards, Washington, DC, 1993.

National Society of Fund-Raising Executives (NSFRE), Alexandria, VA. (Check local and state chapters for workshops and materials).

"1997 Institutional Student Aid Executive Summary," National Association of College and University Business Officers, Washington, DC, 1997.

CHAPTER SIX

Developing the Effective Board

[The fall of 1996] was an autumn to savor, not so much because the Yankees won a World Championship, as because so many of them seemed to be involved in the process.

— *Roger Angell*

As a trustee, you contribute and ask others to give so that the school can fulfill its mission. You exercise your fiduciary responsibilities and monitor the use of all resources. A major resource of any school is the trustees. You work to assure the effectiveness of the board and the success of the school in future years by being involved in bringing potential trustees to the attention of the committee on trustees and by taking advantage of opportunities to develop your own board skills. You not only welcome board members from diverse backgrounds and perspectives, you celebrate such diversity because it opens a multitude of possibilities for the life of the school and board. As a trustee, you are a guardian of the school's well being now and in the future.

❖ *After four meetings I have never seen trustee Jones.*

Importance of the Committee on Trustees

Each and every trustee is critical to the effective functioning of the board. If the board, in concert with the head, constitutes the school's leadership, then every board seat should be filled by competent and committed individuals who give of his or her time, talents, and treasure. If this idea seems self-evident, then why do you find boards with many trustees chronically absent from board and committee meetings, unwilling to give or get, or just disconnected from the work of the board?

A strong committee on trustees is not the only solution to these problems, but it is a major part of the solution to trustee ineffectiveness. This committee, known as the nominating committee in the past, now has a larger, more significant role. Along with the board chair and head, it can bring about and sustain a dynamic, productive board over time. In fact, the committee on trustees is the most critical committee of the board and, no matter how board experts suggest boards should be organized, they all recommend that boards have an active committee on trustees (board development, governance, or nominating committee).

Time commitment

❖ *Isn't the committee on trustees a great committee for those with little time to give to board work?*

The committee on trustees is a year-round, hardworking committee whose goal is to assure the best possible leadership for the school, today and in the years ahead. Because this committee is so important, its members should be recognized by the board and school community as individuals who put the best interest of the school ahead of personal and professional concerns or biases. Some committees are elected by the board, but most are appointed by the chair of the board or by the chair in consultation with the executive committee. Most schools have only trustees serving as committee members; others may have past trustees, nonboard parents and alumnae/i, nonschool leaders (such as educators from other institutions), or any combination of such people. The head and board chair should be active participants on the committee, serving as ex-officio members. However the committee is constituted, it should have members exhibiting the following characteristics:

◆ Commitment to the school's mission

◆ Knowledge of the school — its program, problems, and leadership needs

◆ Knowledge of what constitutes good governance

◆ Personal support of the school's fund development activities

◆ Independence from board and school factions

◆ Willingness and ability to evaluate sitting trustees and potential board members fairly and candidly

◆ Ability to keep committee discussions in confidence

◆ Willingness to make contacts, interview, and recruit new trustees

◆ Respect for other trustees

Relationship to the board and school community

❖ *Can't we leave this trustee selection to the committee?*

The committee on trustees cannot act in isolation. It must reach out to every trustee and other members of the school community for assistance in building the very best board. The committee cannot identify every potential trustee by itself; it needs others to open doors and often to make the actual request for someone to serve as a trustee. The board needs to be involved in setting the criteria for trustees through participation in an annual or biannual self-assessment and in strategic planning that defines the school's current concerns. These activities will define the skills and experiences needed to achieve institutional goals.

Bylaws and Committee on Trustees

❖ *You mean all this is in the bylaws?*

The school's bylaws set forth who should serve on the committee on trustees, whether they are appointed or elected, what the members' terms are, and how the committee chair is selected. Continuity is one of the critical characteristics of an effective committee on trustees. This goal can be achieved by having two- or three-year staggered terms, with some members continuing and others leaving each year.

The bylaws also state the number of trustees on the board, how they are nominated and elected, what their responsibilities are, and how long their terms are. It is recommended that there be specified terms, with a limit on the number of terms a trustee may serve (two three- or four-year terms, three three-year terms, etc.). Bylaws often state that a trustee who has reached his/her last term must leave the board for one year before being eligible for re-election. This rotation brings fresh perspectives to the board's deliberations. However, it can be very helpful to a school to keep a valuable trustee close to the school and invite him/her back after the year's hiatus. If past trustees are kept connected, they can be the best advocates for, and generous funders of, the school.

Committee on Trustees Responsibilities

❖ *Wow! This is real work!*

A committee on trustees needs to meet throughout the year, if it is to accomplish all of its responsibilities. No longer is it appropriate, if it ever was, for the committee to meet two months before the slate is to be presented at the annual board meeting, ask if anyone knows anyone who could possibly serve, and then cajole friends to be trustees as a personal favor, guaranteeing "you just have to show up for a few meetings." Service on the committee on trustees is a major governance role for trustees, as it truly shapes the future of the school.

A note on boarding schools

A boarding school's committee on trustees, because its members are dispersed all over the country and beyond, will need to use modern communication technology. Although such communication can be expensive, it is worth the effort to assure that the committee can accomplish its work in a deliberate and thoughtful manner. Keep in mind that, as a rule, a trustee who is committed to the school and its mission, and for whom the school is a top priority, will be more effective than one who has good board skills, but little commitment.

Tasks of the committee on trustees

The following are the basic tasks for a committee on trustees. (See p. 106 for a sample job description.)

◆ Trustee self-assessment of the strengths and weaknesses of the board and of their own performance.

◆ Assessment of individual trustees. (This is only one example of many that demonstrate how important it is for committee and all board members to keep discussions confidential.)

◆ Exit interviews with departing trustees.

- ◆ Review of school's strategic goals and major strategies to discover what skills, experiences, and relationships are needed for the board today and in the future.

- ◆ Review of demographics of current board. A grid of the demographics, skills, occupations, etc. can be very helpful because an examination of the gaps on the grid can focus the committee on the characteristics the board is lacking and thus should be sought in new trustees. (A generic example of a grid can be found at the end of the chapter.) It is important that a committee on trustees adds characteristics that are especially important to its board. Ethnic, religious, racial, economic, and constituency diversity rightly are of increasing importance to boards.

- ◆ Provide a summary of the board self-assessment to the board.

Former Trustees

❖ *Should we seek theadvice of former trustees?*

Far too many schools spend far too little time and attention on former trustees. It's a mistake to ignore them. In many schools, the head and board chair send all former trustees one or two special updates each year and invite them to former trustees-only parties and special state of the school briefings. In addition, some schools ask former trustees to chair the annual giving fund, auctions, or other special events and, in some cases, capital campaigns.

Honorary Trustees

In the past many schools created special post-trustee categories. It's understandable why schools would do this, but some schools have reported problems having these honorary trustees attend board meetings. Their presence can often impede the work of the board. Yet the advice of former trustees with broad institutional memory can be invaluable. Schools that have had success with former trustees serving in an honorary capacity should obviously continue the practice. Other schools should consider finding alternative ways to sustain the contact and to maintain good relationships with talented former trustees. One way is to form an association of former board chairs. It can function as an advisory committee to the head of school, meeting once or twice a year with the head. This is particularly valuable to new school heads.

Advisory councils

Advisory councils have been effective in some schools, but have caused trouble in others. Problems occur when the group has no clear purpose or mandate, or when the group sees its goals as differing from the goals of the board. Ambiguity doesn't help a school reach its goals. Schools that have success with advisory councils should continue to use them. But a school should think carefully before initiating one. The key concern is whether or not such a group is helping the school reach its goals.

Other Elements of an Effective Board

Develop and communicate candidate criteria and solicit nominations

❖ *Can't we just be glad anyone will serve?*

◆ Develop a list of critical criteria for new trustees, based on a thorough assessment of the board's and school's needs.

◆ Check out the criteria with the board by mail or at a meeting. (This, along with the self-assessment results summary, will keep the board informed on the committee's goals and will prime them to be the committee's partners in the building of the board.)

◆ Communicate the finalized criteria to the board and solicit nominations from the board. Consider including administrators, faculty, parents, and alumnae/i in on the process, making sure that they understand and support the criteria.

◆ Continuously add to the candidate pool and encourage trustees to be ever vigilant in their identification of potential board members.

◆ Ask for specific information on candidates from nominators. Do they meet the criteria? Have they been effective trustees elsewhere? What strengths would they bring to this board? Are they willing to contribute financial support consistent with the school's expectations of trustees and their means? Can they commit the necessary time? Do they support the school's mission? Why do they think they would make effective trustees?

◆ Some committees on trustees seek nominations from individuals outside the immediate school community, such as funders, educators, community leaders, etc.

◆ The larger the pool of candidates, the more the committee on trustees can be assured that their selections will make the very best trustees.

Identify candidates for the board

Based on the criteria and nominating information, rank the candidates. If major gaps exist between the candidate pool and the criteria, renew efforts to increase the pool. Keep a record of all those nominated, along with the information on them so that succeeding committees can review these candidates. A person who might not fit the current criteria might be perfect for the board three years later.

Boards in the process of considering potential trustees sometimes find themselves in the awkward position of deciding not to invite an individual who was led to believe he or she would be asked. To avoid this problem, consider the following:

◆ Make it clear that no one is to contact potential trustees, even to inquire if they are interested in being considered. They can always say no when and if the time comes.

◆ The committee should do as much quiet investigation as possible, resulting in a "short list."

◆ Only those on the short list should be contacted directly, and it should be made clear at the outset that the discussion is exploratory and that the individual should not expect that it will necessarily lead to an invitation to join the board.

Cultivate candidates

❖ *If we tell them everything, they won't want to serve.*

◆ Establish a cultivation/recruitment plan for each candidate and recognize that not every candidate is ready to be a trustee the first time the idea is proposed. It may take one or two years to actually make the "ask."

◆ Select the best person to make the initial contact with the candidate to ascertain her or his interest. Usually this person is the nominator, but he could be the board chair, the committee chair, or a member of the committee. Remember, this is only an initial contact, not the actual request for board service.

◆ Send materials (board job description and requirements, school's strategic plan, etc.) to a candidate once he or she has indicated an interest.

◆ Hold a face-to-face meeting with the candidate. The individual who made the contact, the committee on trustees' chair, and the head should be involved in the meeting. (Heads have many demands on their time, and they may not always be able to attend. However, the work of cultivating and educating trustees is one of the prime responsibilities of a head.) This is the time to discuss time commitment, attendance, and financial expectations of board members. Explain the issues facing the school and the board's role in addressing them and how she/he could add value to the school and the board. Candor is critical; respect the candidate and fully inform her and him. "Recruiters" are concerned that if they tell candidates the full truth, whether it be about the time and financial requirements or school issues, they will frighten them off from serving. It is better for potential trustees to decide not to serve, than it is for them to feel betrayed after joining the board and then learning the real story. Such a situation can even lead to an early resignation from the board. Schools need trustees who are fully committed, and it is better for all concerned to discover that level of commitment up front.

NOTE: Face-to-face meetings, such as described above, can be very difficult for boarding schools. Conference calls could be a substitute if an in-person meeting is impossible.

Recruitment

After the committee on trustees agrees on the slate of nominees, the chair or board chair should contact each nominee to ask him or her to join the board.

Renominate eligible candidates

❖ Don't we always "re-up" everyone for a second term?

◆ If the board leadership is committed to a high-performing board, the charge to the committee on trustees should include a mandate to examine each sitting trustee's eligibility for renomination to another term. The committee considers whether the trustee has fulfilled all trustee expectations and added value to the board.

◆ Current board members who have not met stated requirements should be thanked for their service and not be renominated.

◆ Those trustees who have been effective board members should be contacted by the chair of the committee to thank them for their many contributions and ask them to serve another term.

Nominate officers

❖ Why shouldn't he be chair? He deserves to be after being on the board all these years.

◆ All potential officers need to be very carefully evaluated. While automatic succession from vice chair to chair or chair-elect to chair provides continuity of leadership, occasional circumstances can arise where such succession would be damaging to the school and the life of the board. So it is helpful to have an "out" in the bylaws to handle such a situation.

◆ Officers may be sought for their skills, such as financial expertise for a treasurer, but leadership qualities, commitment to the mission, ability to build consensus, and a broad knowledge of the school are critical for all officers.

◆ The selection of the chair is the paramount decision of the committee on trustees. The chair should be the model for all trustees to emulate and a person whom trustees, administrators, faculty, and parents respect. The chair must view her/himself as the "manager" of the board, just as the head manages the staff. A chair must be committed to teamwork and able to work collegially with the head. The head must get along with the chair. The chair is not required to get along with the head, although it behooves the chair to do so because the partnership of chair and head sets the example for board/head and board/staff relationship. If the chair and the head have problems with each other, disaster almost always follows. It is nearly impossible for a board chair to be "fired," as boards appear willing to wait out a board chair's term rather then asking him/her to step down from office. (For more information on the board/ head relationship see Chapter 7.) A list of desired officer characteristics can be found on p. 111.

❖ *Why ask their opinion? They're not going to be around next year.*

Exit interviews

No matter how trustees leave the board, retirement or resignation, exit interviews should be held in person or over the phone. These interviews should include the following questions:

◆ What did they like about their board service?

◆ What didn't they like about their service?

◆ What are the strengths of the board?

◆ What are the weaknesses and how can they be improved?

◆ What are the strengths of the school?

◆ What are the weaknesses of the school and how could they be improved?

◆ What are the major issues facing the school (different from the weaknesses) and how can the board address them?

◆ What do you know now that you wish you had known sooner?

◆ Is there anything else you would like to tell the board?

◆ Is there some way you would like to continue to work for the school, post-trustee status?

A summary of these interviews, with individual responses kept confidential, should be shared with the board as a part of the committee on trustees' assessment process.

Select members of the committee on trustees

For committee member qualifications see pp. 82-83.

Present trustee and officer slate, as well as slate of committee of trustees members, if applicable

◆ The slate, with bios or résumés, is sent to the board usually by a specified time before the annual meeting.

◆ Most often a single slate of nominees is proposed. Bylaws can provide a method to propose additional nominees beyond the official slate, with requirements for notification to the committee on trustees by a defined date and an agreement of additional nominees to have their names put forward for election.

◆ The election is held.

◆ The board chair or committee on trustees' chair contacts newly-elected trustees, welcomes them to the board, and tells them when and where the orientation will be held.

◆ Sitting trustees are assigned to be mentors to new board members. The mentors should contact the new trustees shortly after their notification of their election. This relationship should continue for at least a year so that the newcomer has someone to turn to for advice and information on the underlying issues and relationships that are part of every board's life. All mentors should have similar or parallel agendas or topics to address with new trustees, though the manner in which they offer help will naturally vary.

Board orientation

❖ *Why take so much valuable time to orient new trustees? They'll pick it up as they go along.*

As soon as possible, hold a rigorous board orientation that delineates:

◆ School's mission

◆ Board roles, responsibilities, and performance expectations

◆ Board's relationship to the head and the rest of the staff

◆ Board organizational structure and operating procedures, policies, and other major documents

◆ Information on the school's history, finances, fund-raising activities, program, students, etc.

◆ Goals of the current strategic plan

◆ Mail the board manual (list of suggested contents can be found on p. 104) before the orientation or hand out at the orientation. Remember, this is a massive amount of material for anyone to digest. Do not expect new trustees to grasp all of the nuances of governance, the ramifications of the strategic plan, etc. at the orientation. It will take time and ongoing mentoring for trustees to be fully oriented. A board manual cannot substitute for a live orientation. If it is very difficult to schedule a group orientation, the chair of the committee on trustees and the chair of the board, and the head, if available, should meet individually with new trustees who cannot make the formal orientation session.

◆ The board chair and head should take leading roles at the formal orientation; other appropriate trustees and staff should be present. However, a long list of presenters can overwhelm trustees. Also, allow lots of time for questions.

◆ Many boards supply all new trustees with their own copy of this *Trustee Handbook*, with the suggestion that they read it in advance of the orientation.

Board development

❖ *What do you mean there should be a line item in the budget for board development?*

The best boards regularly pause in their work in order to advance their own training and knowledge, to better serve their schools. Examples of professional development for boards include workshops on governance, often led by experienced outside facilitators; presentations on current issues and challenges facing the school; presentations on demographics, diversity, technology; joint meetings/workshops with trustees from other schools.

Retention

◆ The key to retention is to involve all trustees in areas where they can add value and in which they are interested. It is critical to include new trustees quickly in the work of the board, especially if they were recruited for expressed reasons.

◆ Board meetings need to be focused on major strategic issues. Sufficient time should be scheduled for in-depth discussions of these issues which then leads to decisions, whether by consensus or a vote. (See Chapter 10 for more information on board meetings.)

◆ Provide for trustees to be educated or trained by budgeting resources and time to do so. Trustees' personal development will add to the effectiveness of the board as a whole.

◆ Maintain a warm, open climate that welcomes diversity in individuals and their backgrounds, experiences, styles of thinking, etc.

◆ It is a responsibility of the board chair to be open, engaging, and accessible to all trustees.

Recognition

❖ *Another plaque?*

Even though trustees say they do not need to be recognized because they serve the school for which they care so deeply, do not believe them; they love recognition!

◆ Plan a formal recognition for those who leave the board. Plaques are nice, but mementos that demonstrate personal thought went into their selection are even better. Student letters or pictures can make great gifts.

◆ Consider a yearly award/honor to a board member who exemplifies the very best attributes of effective trusteeship. Do not give only to officers.

◆ Encourage the board chair and head to informally recognize trustees for board and personal achievements all during the year, whether at meetings, by notes, or other inventive means.

Trustee Diversity

❖ *I'm comfortable with this board as it is. Why change?*

Boards of trustees have an increasing commitment to diversity in their student body, faculty, and administration. When it comes to the diversity of the board itself, boards often struggle to include trustees of various ethnic, religious, and socioeconomic groups. This should be a case of "Do as I do" as well as "Do as I say" because the board should be the model of moral leadership in this area, as it should be in all areas. If a school states that it is committed to diversity, its board should reflect and honor the pluralism of the school and its community. As noted in the NAIS *Principles of Good Practice for Equity and Justice*, "Schools have found that the process of creating and sustaining an equitable and just community requires commitment, reflection, conscious and deliberate action, as well as constant vigilance."

The following are some steps that might be helpful as you work toward a more heterogeneous board.

◆ Be sure the board chair, head, and chair of committee on trustees agree that a more diverse board is critical to the ultimate effectiveness of the board and that they will exercise strong, visible leadership on the issue.

◆ Hold a board conversation on the issue and discuss questions such as:

Does our board composition reflect the community we serve? Does it reflect the kind of community the school wishes to become?

Do certain constituencies lack a voice at the board table?

Are we missing perspectives that could expand our thinking in new ways?

How can we move beyond tokenism?

NOTE: *If there are a few people of color, or of a religious faith that is a minority population in the school, do not expect those members of the board to speak for a group. Expect them to speak as any trustee might.*

◆ Develop a plan for change. This responsibility usually falls to the committee on trustees, but with their many responsibilities, this could be the perfect place for a task force organized to develop the plan and guide the board in its implementation. Outside consultants can be of assistance because they have expertise in diversity and change issues and are objective.

◆ Take advantage of community leadership programs and professional and service associations, especially those that involve diverse populations. Such organizations are often willing and even eager to place their members on boards.

◆ Talk to community leaders and ask for their suggestions.

◆ Try to get a number of less traditional trustees at one time and assign mentors to them who are experienced trustees and committed to making diversity work for the board. Involve the new trustees quickly in board work where they can contribute their talents.

◆ Once the new trustees are on board, truly welcome them and the new perspectives they may bring to the board table. Celebrate the fresh ideas, problem-solving skills, and resources that are part of your trustee team.

❖ *What do*
we mean by
diversity?

Defining diversity and multiculturalism

Schools tend to use the word "diversity" to mean both "diversity" and "multiculturalism." This is fine, though it can be helpful to consider the difference between the two.

Diversity simply describes the various constituents of a group. It's quantitative. Most obviously, it is defined by race, gender, and culture (or ethnicity). On a more subtle level it includes class, sexual orientation, religion, disability, and even appearance. But the list can be as varied as a school deems necessary and right. It is helpful to pause and reflect on the many forms of diversity:

race
gender
socioeconomic status
national origin
physical ability/disability
ethnicity
politics
culture
family structure
sexual orientation
constituency (parents, alumnae/i, faculty, students, past parents, funders, friends)
geographic area of residence
age
marital status
religion
values
mental ability
…and on and on

Multiculturalism is generally considered to be an evolving process. Diversity is quantitative, whereas multiculturalism is qualitative. It is the shift that occurs when we move from defining everyone by one cultural norm to an understanding of the value of multiple norms. To put it another way, a multicultural community is one that embraces diversity, that believes the community is stronger, more equitable and more just specifically because of its diversity.

Constituencies

When considering new members for the board of trustees, most boards
focus on the constituencies these potential new board members represent.
In considering bringing in new members based on their constituency, you
should be aware of the following.

Parents

Day school boards tend to have large numbers of trustee-parents. Often
K–6 and K–8 school boards are made up exclusively of parents. Cooperative
school boards are by definition boards constituted solely of parents. Parents
bring a deep personal interest in the school. However, they can be focused
too much on the present, generalize from their children's experiences, and
become more involved in operational matters than they should be.

Alumnae/i

Day school boards of K–12 and secondary schools have more alumnae/i
trustees. Boarding schools often have a majority of graduates as trustees.
Alumnae/i board members bring a spirit of gratitude for their education and
are living examples of the fulfillment of the school's mission. Occasionally
they are so enamored of the past that they have difficulty adapting to and
embracing change.

Faculty

A small percentage of schools have faculty-trustees. This is not a recommended practice, but many schools that have faculty on the board find them
to be deeply committed to the school's mission, bringing their educational
expertise and knowledge of students to the board's deliberations. However,
most boards look to the head for such expertise and knowledge. In fact,
faculty-trustees are their own "bosses," as the board oversees the head, who
oversees the faculty. This conflict of interest can make things very difficult.

Students

Very few schools have students as trustees. Not only are they not of age legally, but their general maturity can make it difficult for them to move beyond
their particular experiences as a current student. There are occasional exceptions to this wisdom, but there are ways to involve students in the work of

the board, without electing them to it. Some ways boards involve students are service on committees, meetings of trustees with student leaders, surveys on their interests, etc.

Past Parents

These individuals may constitute the best of all worlds for trustee service: commitment, knowledge, and distance from current school issues. Grandparents may offer similar perspectives.

Funders

While it is hoped that all adult school constituents contribute funds to the school, it is not recommended that representatives from private and corporate foundations serve on the board. Many foundations have policies that forbid employees from serving on boards of institutions they do or may fund. There can be a perceived or real conflict of interest for such individuals to serve as trustees.

Friends

These trustees can bring the most objectivity and needed expertise not found within the immediate school community to board deliberations. They may require more in-depth orientation to the school than other trustees.

Whew! That is an incredible committee agenda, but it is imperative that boards assure their own high standard of performance because it will continue their schools' excellence over the years to come. This is why the committee on trustees is so important.

As a trustee, no matter your background or connections, you mentor new board members, making all feel welcomed and valued. You listen attentively to your fellow trustees' opinions, honoring their viewpoints. You are open to new ideas, and present your own opinions with candor and tact. While you take your board work seriously, you should also not take yourself too seriously. You look for opportunities to bring appropriate humor to discussions, recognizing that a little levity can ease tense situations — and that joy and laughter are very important elements in the health of the school community.

DIMENSIONS OF AN EFFECTIVE BOARD

The following is a list of "Board Competencies" that make for an effective, well-functioning board. Reprinted with permission from *The Effective Board of Trustees* by Richard P. Chait, et al.

1. Contextual Dimension

The board understands the institution's mission, tradition, and history and the board's behaviors are consistent with institutional values.

2. Educational Dimension

The board emphasizes the need to learn, seek feedback on board performance, and to provide the opportunity for trustee education and self reflection.

3. Interpersonal Dimension

The board nurtures the development of trustees as a group, establishes group goals, and consciously attends to the board's collective strength and welfare.

4. Intellectual Dimension

The board recognizes complexities, tolerates ambiguities, sees trustees as one constituency among many, and understands how different issues, actions and decisions affect one another.

5. Political Dimension

The board respects and guards the integrity of the governance process, avoids win-lose situations, accepts as one of its primary responsibilities the need to build healthy relationships among key constituencies.

6. Strategic Dimension

The board directs its attention to a few priorities or decisions identified as having strategic or symbolic importance to the institution.

CASE STUDY

What's Past Is ... Our Problem Now

In a rush to fill a vacant board position, trustees at River Academy, an institution highly sensitive to its students of color (40 percent of the student population), hurriedly approve the nomination of Bill Smith, who recently expanded his sporting goods business into River's surrounding community. During a subsequent trip to Bill's hometown, one trustee became distraught when she discovered that Bill was a former youth leader of a white supremacist group. The board's bylaws do not allow for a member's removal unless that member "demonstrates behavior detrimental to the well-being of River Academy or any of its students, faculty, or staff." Since his appointment to the board Smith has maintained a very low profile, so he does not fall under the provisions of termination.

What are the issues?

What should the committee on trustees do?

What should the board do?

What should the board chair do?

What should Bill Smith do?

What should the head do?

SAMPLE MATERIALS

Board Manual Contents

Board membership and calendar

◆ List of trustees with names, preferred addresses for mail and e-mail, preferred phone and fax numbers, short biographies

◆ Board and committee job descriptions

◆ List of officers, with titles

◆ Committee lists, including names and addresses of non-trustee members

◆ Calendar of board, committee meetings, and any other meetings or function at which trustee attendance is expected — for the fiscal/administrative year

Organizational background information

◆ Mission, vision, and philosophy statements

◆ Short history of the school, including how it was established, major events, and individuals involved at critical decision points

◆ Description of the total program

◆ Description of the student body

◆ Strategic plan

◆ Most recent annual report

◆ Public relations material, especially those items describing the school's program and facilities

◆ Organizational chart

Bylaws and policies

◆ Articles of incorporation, corporate charter, and bylaws

◆ Board policies on conflicts of interest, attendance at meetings, indemnification/directors and officers liability, reimbursement for expenses, giving and getting, etc.

◆ Public policy statements, if any have been adopted by the board

Administration/Faculty

◆ List of administrators with titles, faculty and staff

◆ Faculty handbook (or where it can be accessed)

◆ Job descriptions of key administrators (or where they can be accessed)

◆ Personnel policies, including evaluation process (or where they can be accessed)

Students

◆ Student handbook

◆ School student/parent list

◆ Two or three issues of the student newspaper

Finances

◆ Financial policies and procedures, including investment policy (or where they can be accessed)

◆ Budget

◆ Long-range financial plan

◆ Most recent independent audit report

◆ Annual fund-raising plan

◆ Periodic financial reports (if separate from minutes)

Minutes and issue descriptions

◆ Minutes of several board meetings

◆ Brief description of issues facing the school, especially those that involve the board

Resources

◆ Bibliography on Trusteeship

◆ Local, State, or Regional Independent School Association

◆ National Association of Independent School (NAIS)

◆ *Trustee Handbook*, NAIS

◆ NAIS *Principles of Good Practice* (for Independent School Trustees, for Boards of Trustees, for Equity and Justice)

NOTE: It is obvious that not all of the above will actually fit in a three-ring binder, but an accordion file can work well to hold much of the extra material. However, a binder for the items to which trustees need to refer most often is very helpful. And make sure it has a pocket big enough to hold the Trustee Handbook!

Committee on Trustees Job Description
(Based on Bylaws)

Purpose:

The committee on trustees determines the composition of the board — identifying, recruiting, and proposing new trustees. The board also facilitates the board's self-assessment; plans for leadership succession; and plans for trustee professional development through orientation, training, and ongoing education.

Tasks:

Review plan for the year.

◆ Facilitate board self-assessment and undertake other assessments/evaluations in order to develop criteria for renomination of sitting members whose terms are up and for nomination of new trustees.

◆ Check criteria with the board and enlist trustees and others to assist with identifying candidates.

◆ Review board recruitment materials.

◆ Identify candidates and make sure that there is sufficient information on each one so that the committee can make reasoned decisions.

◆ Interview likely candidates to ascertain their interest and to begin the education process.

◆ Develop a slate of new trustees, with back-up candidates for each vacancy.

◆ Ask chosen candidates if they will serve.

◆ Present slate of trustees to board for approval.

◆ Plan for the succession of leadership, evaluate current officers, and recommend an officer slate to the board for its approval.

◆ Select members of the committee on trustees (if this is one of the committee's responsibilities).

◆ Orient new trustees and organize continuing education programs that enhance trustees' knowledge of their governance responsibilities, independent school educational issues, and the school's programs and needs.

Members:

As described in the bylaws

Relationship to the Board:

Works closely with the board chair, who serves on the committee ex-officio. Includes the board in the process, especially in the areas of assessment, development of selection criteria, and identification of potential candidates. The full board approves the slates of trustees, officers, and committee on trustees members, if that is part of the committee's charge.

Relationship to the Head:

Works closely with the head, who serves on the committee ex-officio. Seeks advice of head on all aspects of the committee's work. Head should be involved in and have a voice in the meetings with potential trustees and new trustee orientation.

Time Commitment:

Year-round committee, meeting X times per year

Resources:

Board self-assessment tools

Nominating grid

Strategic plan

Orientation information

Bylaws — policies

Diversity goals

Board manual

Trustee expectations

Board Profile Grid

(Schools can create a grid or simply group board members by categories. The point is to get a visual representation of the board's profile.)

Name:

Sex:

Male

Female

Age:

21-35

36-50

51-65

Over 65

Race/Ethnicity:

African American

American Indian/Alaskan Native

Asian or Pacific Islander

Caucasian

Latina/o

Other

Profession:

Arts

Banking

Business owner

Civil service

Corporate

Education: Elementary

Secondary

Higher education

Finance

Human relations

Law

Media

Medicine

Politics

Religion

Social services

Area Of Expertise:

Administration — General

Education

Facilities management

Financial management

Fund-raising

Health care

Information services/technology

Legal affairs

Media/Public relations

Personnel management

Strategic planning

Constituency:

Parent

Alumnae/i

Funder

Other

Additional Characteristics:

Ability to give funds

Willingness to give funds

Connections to people with funds

Connections to people with clout

Time available

Successful experience on other boards

Commitment to process and shared
   decision-making

(The above items are only illustrative. A board-member grid needs to be customized for each school. Sometimes it is most appropriate to only select those items that are truly critical for the board at the time the evaluation is being undertaken.)

Trustee Time and Financial Requirements — A Worksheet

Ongoing Activities	Time Estimates per Month (Adjust for boarding schools)
1. Board meetings	
2. Committee meetings	
3. Fund-raising	
4. Other meetings	
5. Phone calls	
6. Leadership positions (officers, committee chairs, financial campaign chairs, special event chairs, parent association chair, and alumnae/i association chair)	
Seasonal or Time Limited Activities	**Time Estimates per Activity**
1. Fund-raising campaigns	
2. Special events	
3. Issue task forces	
Financial Activites	**Estimated Costs**
1. Annual campaign	
2. Capital campaign	
3. Special events or other fund-raising activities	
4. Hosting events for cultivation of donors, potential trustees,etc.	
5. Board expenses (if not reimbursed)	
• Travel	
• Meals	
• Lodging (boarding schools)	
• Child care	

Officer Qualifications Criteria

Criteria	Name	Name	Name
1. Committed to the schools' mission & vision and goals of strategic plan			
2. Willing to assume responsibility			
3. Able to exercise authority			
4. Able and willing to make decisions, especially within group decision-making process			
5. Knowledgeable about the school			
6. Actively updates governance knowledge and skills			
7. Maintains big picture of the school			
8. Focuses own energy and that of others on policy issues			
9. Sensitive to cliques and power struggles, but is disassociated from them			
10. Delegates responsibility to others			
11. Works to develop potential leaders			
12. Skilled at long-range strategic planning			
13. Able to problem-solve			
14. Effective oral and written communicator			
15. Has basic knowledge of parliamentary procedure and knows how to preside at meetings			
16. Contributes and raises funds			
17. Works well with the head			

This form is not in priority order. It would be appropriate for a committee on trustees to set the priorities that apply to its school. Also, to add qualities/qualifications that are important to its school.

Sample Trustee/School Commitment Letter

Dear Trustee,

As a member of the board of trustees, you are in a position to make a significant contribution to School X and its students. The vitality of the school depends on your commitment and imaginative and caring leadership. In fact, the future well-being of the school is in your hands. You and the other members of the board are trustholders of all that is important to the life of the school and as such need to be clear about your responsibilities. I am asking each trustee to review the following areas of personal commitment:

1. Attend board of trustees meetings held X times a year. Your presence is valued and your active participation is a critical component of board deliberations. Therefore, according to the bylaws, after three unexcused absences, it is assumed that you do not want to serve.

2. Serve on a minimum of one committee or task force. The work of the board is most often accomplished through its committees, and your expertise will help move the board's agenda forward.

3. In order to be an effective trustee, you must read and be familiar with material sent to you in advance of board and committee meetings.

4. Contribute direct financial support to the school. It is expected that 100 percent of the board will contribute to the annual fund and also to any capital/endowment campaigns. Your support tells other potential contributors that our board of trustees is tangibly committed as donors. Trustees serve as key resources for access to other individuals, foundations, and corporations where they have influence.

4. Spend a half a day attending classes in a class or division other than your child's. Visits should be arranged through the head's office. By experiencing the educational process firsthand, trustees become better informed advocates for the school as a whole.

Just as you have responsibilities to the school, you also have the right to expect that the school will fulfill its responsibilities to you as a member of its board of trustees:

1. You can anticipate a judicious and respectful use of your time. The asset of time is one of the most critical resources busy people such as you have. We commit our best to use your time in a manner that will return value to your personal contribution. If we fail in our attempt, please let me know.

2. We will get important information, including meeting agendas, minutes, financial reports, committee updates, and reports requiring action, to you in a timely manner before each meeting. We will also keep you informed about any critical events/concerns that may arise between meetings. Please let me know if the format of reports does not facilitate your participation in the board's work.

Are they too long, too terse, confusing? Can you ask the important questions that need to be asked from the information provided?

3. We will provide you with a thorough orientation to the board and the school and ongoing training and education to assist you in being the most effective trustee you can be.

4. We provide directors and officers liability insurance. If you were to be accused of wrongful acts committed while performing your trustee duties, you are indemnified against reasonable costs of defense proceedings, damages, judgments, and settlement costs up to $xx per occurrence. Wrongful acts covered include making errors in statements or mistaking information, making misleading statements or admissions, performing misleading acts, and neglecting or breaching duties whether proven or accused. The policy does not cover willful negligence or criminal activity.

5. Please feel free to contact me at _____. I do look forward to hearing from you, whether it be with questions or concerns on school/board issues or even praise of school/board accomplishments.

The quality of School X depends upon a committed, knowledgeable, and involved board of trustees. I look forward to serving with you and accomplishing results that will make a difference in the lives of our very special students.

If you concur with these responsibilities, I would appreciate your signature of commitment. Please return one copy to me in the enclosed envelope.

Sincerely,

Jane Doe
Chair of the Board

_____
Signature of trustee

_____
Printed name of trustee

_____
Date

Note: This letter is meant only as an example to be adapted for your school. It's best to have each section reviewed to make sure that it is accurate for your situation. Item #4 concerning officers and directors liability insurance, for instance, needs to be checked against your school's insurance policy.

RESOURCES

Andringa, Robert C. and Ted W. Engstrom, *Nonprofit Board Answer Book*, National Center for Nonprofit Boards, Washington, DC, 1998.

Bailey, Mark, *The Troublesome Board Member,* National Center for Nonprofit Boards, Washington, DC, 1996.

Gale, Robert L., *The Committee on Trustees,* Association of Governing Boards of Universities and Colleges, Washington, DC, 1996.

Johnson, Eric W., *Evaluating the Performance of Trustees and School Heads,* National Association of Independent Schools, Washington, DC, 1986.

"Making Diversity Meaningful in the Boardroom" CarverGuide Series. John Carver. Jossey-Bass, San Francisco, CA, 1997.

Nelson, Judith Grummon, *Six Keys to Recruiting, Orienting, and Involving Nonprofit Board Members,* National Center for Nonprofit Boards, Washington, DC, 1995.

Rutledge, Jennifer M., *Building Board Diversity,* National Center for Nonprofit Boards, Washington, DC, 1994.

Slesinger, Larry, *Self-Assessment for Nonprofit Governing Boards,* National Center for Nonprofit Boards, Washington, DC, 1995 (User's Guide & Individual Board Member Questionnaire).

CHAPTER SEVEN

The Relationship Between the Board and the Head

Power is the capacity to generate relationships.

— *Margaret J. Wheatley*

NOTE: The chair has so many special responsibilities in terms of relationship with the head that this partnership team is the subject of its own chapter, Chapter 8.

As a trustee, you are ever mindful of your shared responsibility, especially in three areas: 1) to help shape strategy and set goals, 2) maximize use of resources, and 3) assure timely evaluation of the work of the board and school.

You understand that the trustees, under the direction of the board chair, work cooperatively with the head, and that the relationship can succeed only through mutual accommodation and trust.

The relationship between the head of school and the board members, collectively and individually, is one of the most important determinants of the strength and the success of the institution. Some of these relationships are formal, others informal, but it is equally important for all parties to be aware of the appropriate guidelines and policies for interaction. Good communication is at the heart of a strong board.

The Formal Relationship

Hiring the head

❖ *Who hires the head?*

The head is hired by the board, collectively. Not by the search chair. Not by the board chair, even though the latter signs the contract. The *entire* board extends the offer of employment, with all its joys and challenges, and supports the head in the important work of the school. Because hiring a head is the most important act the board of a school can do, it is an act that should be done carefully, procedurally, and not too frequently.

A written contract

The board, modeling good practices, offers a written contract to the head, delineating

◆ responsibilities of the head

◆ terms of compensation

◆ evaluation process

◆ term of the contract, renewal and termination provisions

Responsibilities of the head

❖ *What is the essential job of the head?*

These may be generally stated in the contract and amplified in annual goal setting or other supplementary documents. They should indicate that the head is the professional, institutional, and educational leader of the school, and that he or she is authorized to oversee all administration. Other key concepts:

◆ The head works with board and staff to implement board policies.

◆ The head has complete authority for faculty, staff, and student selection, evaluation, and dismissal.

◆ The head keeps the board informed about decisions in all these areas.

◆ The head is responsible with the financial officer, if any, and the treasurer of the board for development and monitoring of the school's resources.

Compensation

Compensation should include cash salary and basic benefits extended to all faculty and staff, and others as the laws allow, which a school is willing to customize according to the head's needs and wishes. The range of compensation covered in NAIS contracts (and over 90 percent of heads now have written contracts) includes insurance and pension contributions, housing assistance, automobile use, vacation and sick leave, including sabbatical provisions, professional development, moving expenses, assistance with school expenses for the head's children and school-related expenses, and includes club and entertainment funds. Many heads also receive extra insurance and deferred compensation. In some schools spouses have separate allowances as well.

Compensation review

❖ *What factors determine head's compensation?*

Heads have different needs as individuals and members of a family, and at different stages of their careers. The board, wishing to retain a head in whom it has placed great hope and faith, and having expended effort and energy in the search, continues to assure an annual compensation review. This is the responsibility of a small group of trustees who have been designated for this purpose, perhaps the chair and the treasurer, or the chair, the chair-elect, and the treasurer. They avail themselves of national and regional resources to assure that the compensation they offer is competitive in their market. To assure a balance of competing and limited resources, they also measure the head's compensation against that of other administrators and staff, in annual "snapshots" and in trends of growth over time.

Evaluation

❖ *Why all this bother about evaluation?*

The board, with the head, sets annual goals for the head's performance and for its own, and is organized to conduct annual evaluations in three areas:

◆ the head of school

◆ the board itself

◆ the board leadership, especially the chair

Evaluations are based on mutually agreed upon goals set in advance of the school year, and measured some months later, often in late spring, before setting new goals for the coming year. Ordinarily these evaluations are submitted, according to the agreed-upon format, only to the trustees. Other evaluations, by parents, students, and faculty, are not the norm in independent schools, but they are growing in number. Where desired, they can offer useful input. The bottom line is that head evaluation — as head hiring and support — is the board's responsibility and head evaluation is ultimately the responsibility for the board and the board alone.

Evaluation and goals

❖ *Should an evaluation be linked to goals?*

The evaluation process must be based on mutually-established goals and a mutually established process known and made clear in advance to all parties. It is important for head and board both to know what the focus of the year's work will be — for, in fact, the priorities and tasks will vary from year to year according to where a school is in the cycle of the head's tenure, its capital campaign, etc.

While the provisions and details of the evaluation process do not need to be included in the contract, NAIS recommends that the topic be addressed there; the same could be true for the head's responsibilities, which could be expanded in a separate document. But to indicate that evaluation — of head, board and board leadership — will be a regular and ongoing part of the work of the school is too important to leave to a later date. Do not say, "It's June, let's evaluate the head some way." Goals and evaluation are the central measure of the head and board's work. They are too important to leave to chance, anecdotal reporting, or last-minute planning. Open-ended, last-minute evaluations not based on previously set goals are not fair to the head or the school, and unlikely to reflect its mission.

Compensation and evaluation

Some "experts" like to keep the discussion of compensation unlinked to evaluation, but in reality it is very difficult to do so. Therefore, some boards tie a portion of discretionary compensation to evaluation.

❖ *How should the evaluation be shared with the board? With the head?*

Sharing the results of evaluations

The board chair should share the results of the evaluation with the full board in executive session, taking the opportunity to reflect on strengths and weaknesses and to indicate priorities for the coming year. This sharing should be in general terms.

It is important that the chair and others on the head's evaluation committee or as designated, meet with the head to share more fully the overall results of the evaluation. It is appropriate that they, or at least the chair, meet with the head both before and after the executive session meeting.

Term of contract, renewal and termination

❖ *Should we offer a one-year contract or a multiple-year contract?*

Finally, the contract should spell out clearly its duration. Multiple-year contracts are the norm for many heads in today's world, and can be advantageous to both parties to the agreement. With a beginning head, particularly in a first-year headship, a school may wish to extend a one-year contract before providing for multiple years, but in recent years many new heads are being offered multiple-year contracts as they enter the position.

The most common form of multiple-year contract is a three-year one, with annual rollover provisions. In offering a multiple-year contract, a school indicates it is committed to the head's leadership for that period and perhaps beyond. Continuity of leadership is a valuable commodity and such terms are a strong statement of support for a head. The expectation is that the head will honor the commitment and stay focused on the school's priorities for that term. In reality, however, some heads have been tempted by other opportunities and such agreements are, in essence, more binding on the school than on the head.

Renewal of contract

It is important to establish an annual timetable for contract renewal talks, even in the middle of a three-year cycle. Compensation will change from year to year, as will annual goals. It is easier for a head to offer contracts to faculty and staff if the head's own next year's contract and terms are safely accomplished, so mid-school year is a frequent date to complete the agreement for next year's contract. June, following evaluation, is another.

Advantages of multiple-year contracts

Multiple-year contracts with financial obligation to the school help the school retain a vital ingredient of the strong and healthy school: continuity of leadership. They help the head know the board's commitment and willingness to work together. They also help protect the board from pressures of trustees who hold as their models the high tech, corporate turnover rate. In a number of the unplanned departures of heads in recent years, there has been an underlying factor of trustees who urge the head's departure at the first mistake. Disasters have followed such precipitate decisions, more so for school and board than for the departing head. Multiple-year contracts can let cooler heads prevail, all in the best interests of the school, and help assure that change, when necessary, is planned.

Terms for premature departure of the head at the will of the board

❖ *Can't we just deal with this when trouble arises?*

Inclusion of provisions for termination in every contract, a situation all hope will never occur, is important for both head and board. The best time to put the terms in writing is at the optimistic start of the new relationship. Unplanned departures can be disruptive to school enrollment, faculty morale, community perceptions, and fund-raising. A well-run and well-led board is unlikely to suffer this problem, and careful attention to the many parts of this handbook will help schools avoid such an occurrence. But the situations do occur and, sadly, sometimes recur. They are easier to resolve when the terms are clearly spelled out well in advance.

There are several reasons to put these terms in writing in the contract. All offer protection to the head, the board, and the broader school community. A board that does not give consideration to this aspect of its own professionalism — i.e., possibly letting go a head with no departure package, not for cause but because the board decided late in the year they would like to seek new leadership — risks not attracting strong and committed candidates in the next search. Who would want to go to a school that treated its last head like that? A precipitate, unplanned, uncompensated departure may also result in a qualified accreditation report. A school that does not allow for best practices, even in one of the worst of situations, is probably not living up to its own mission statement and what it says about how the school values and treats members of its community.

A school must also protect its own interests, especially financial ones. Model three-year contracts are not commitments to compensate for three years if the head is asked by the board to leave before that period ends. Because of possible unforeseen changes in plans, multiple-year contracts usually stipulate that if the board gives notice before December 1 or January 1 of the present school year, the contract will not be renewed. A head, then, has a short, but reasonable time to seek new employment. If the board gives notice after January 1 — that is, after the date many searches at other schools are well advanced or complete — the agreement should include a full year's salary and other benefits, as determined, in compensation for the unplanned termination.

Heads have a responsibility to give adequate advance notice of departure as well. A year's notice allows the school ample time to launch and complete a successful search. Ordinarily, a head voluntarily leaving before completing of a multi-year contract would not receive compensation for any time under contract that he or she does not serve.

As a trustee, you understand that clearly stated basic terms and expectations in each of these four categories are the backbone of a good contract and provide the foundation for a solid relationship with the head.

A final word about head's contract and compensation

The full board, in executive session, needs to know the basic parameters of the head's contract. "We have extended the head's contract through the year 2002, subject to annual review of performance, to include a raise in salary within the 4–6 percent guidelines for all faculty and staff." Other details to include the actual terms of salary and benefits need only be known to a smaller group of trustees who comprise the head's compensation committee. The chair, treasurer, and perhaps the chair-elect are a normal model.

Other reasons for executive sessions

❖ *You have mentioned executive session for the head's contract and evaluation. Are there other occasions when the board should meet alone?*

There is no single answer to this question. It used to be that boards never met without the head present, but lately, taking the model used by other nonprofits, especially colleges and universities, a number of boards meet regularly in executive session at the end of each meeting, for no more than fifteen minutes, often less. The purpose is to get a general sense of how things are going, and to get the sense that the board is doing all it can to support the head.

Many people, especially a large number of heads, are very uncomfortable with this concept and it is certainly nothing to enter into without full agreement of all parties as to the limited purpose of the meeting. It takes a skillful, experienced chair and other board leaders, as well as a head who has full confidence that the chair will let him know the gist of the meeting the very next day. "We think we have asked you to be on the road too much and want to review your schedule of capital campaign travels." "Now that your daughter has gone on to college, could you aim to balance your visits to both middle and upper school lacrosse games?"

A minority of schools do this as a matter of course. Each school should decide its own modes of operation only after serious and candid discussion with all affected parties.

Areas Where Formal and Informal Relationships Overlap

Other relationships for all trustees with the head are delineated in NAIS's *Principles of Good Practice for Independent School Trustees*. These are a set of principles distinct from the *Principles of Good Practice for Boards*. They govern conduct for individual trustees and cover many of the areas that are often not clearly delineated, that fall between formal and informal relationships of trustees with the head of school.

Principles of Good Practice for Trustees

An individual trustee does not become involved in specific management, personnel, or curricular issues.

Of course individual trustees from time to time may wish to share with the head their perceptions of a candidate for the school, either a student or teacher, or to offer the view that Spanish rather than French would seem to be the right language for elementary students in the 21st century, or that the soccer coach seems to be losing heart for her job. The key word here is *involved*.

Once individual trustees' thoughts are shared with the head, their resolution should be referred to the proper committee. The faculty, and the board committee on education may wish to hear more about the Spanish-French topic, but the final decision lies with the school and its professional educators. The same concept should underlie all admission, evaluation, and dismissal decisions, concerning either students or staff.

NOTE: *An independent school board should not act as a court of review or a court of last resort in discipline, dismissal, or termination cases. A trustee whose agenda is overly full of advice in these areas should be spoken to by the board chair, who is the proper disciplinarian of the board. It is not a role for a head to undertake, nor is it the head's responsibility.*

A trustee accepts and supports board decisions and respects board confidentiality.

Support for decisions:

❖ *What if I disagree with a board decision?*

The board can only operate as a collective entity: one board, one decision, one voice. This precept does not mean that trustees cannot disagree in the course of decision-making. It is to be hoped that a strong board includes people of different views who will regularly consider alternative points of view with courtesy and respect, and support decisions carefully researched and debated once consensus has been reached.

After discussion and debate, all trustees are expected to support decisions. If they cannot — i.e., a military school or a single-sex school decides to change its mission and several alumni/ae cannot support that decision — then they should resign from the board. Resignations should be accepted with gratitude and understanding. At a later date, the former trustee may be just the person to return to the board when he or she has had time to see the effects of the new decision in action. But to have a trustee stating views contrary to the board's official decision is invariably damaging to the school as it goes forward on its new course.

If the board has reviewed the performance of a head and decided that firm goals will be in place for the coming year to give the head time to address perceived weaknesses in leadership, every trustee has the obligation to keep details of the agreement confidential and to give the head support, both public and private, as the school moves forward. Again, if the trustee cannot agree to give both public and private support in such a situation, resignation is the proper response.

Confidentiality:

❖ *Can't I just tell my spouse and family?*

It is important to remember that we live today in a culture that in many ways does not respect confidentiality. Our schools are not immune to the expectation that everything can and should be known by everybody.

Especially in day schools, with so many current parents in the immediate community and on the board, there is a natural tendency to share confidential topics with spouses or partners. A good board chair will help work against this tendency with frequent reminders of the need for confidentiality, beginning with orientation of new trustees, and especially when sensitive matters become the subject for board dialogue. It may help for trustees to ask themselves before discussing board matters, "Does this person have a need to know what I know?" The answer, almost invariably, is "no."

A trustee takes care to separate the interests of the school from the interests of a particular child or constituency.

❖ *How could the school reject my daughter? Don't trustees get special privileges?*

A trustee may often be tempted to lobby for "all third grade parents" or "alumni/ae from the seventies," but should also remember once she is a trustee she speaks for all constituencies, not a particular one.

A trustee may also be tempted to lobby for a particular or potential constituent, possibly the admission or hiring of someone to whom she is connected. These impulses are natural, and a wise head expects them. But the trustee, having made the case for a candidate, should then leave the decision with the institution and respect even the decisions that are hardest to swallow. A trustee whose child, after due process, has been suspended or expelled from school, may be tempted to leave the board or to withdraw a campaign pledge, but it is also possible that the trustee will want to continue to support the school, agreeing with the decision and the process.

Similar logic is necessary when a school must deny a place to the child of a trustee. The trustee must have confidence in the admission policies and process. If the answer is no, the qualified members of the school community have determined that the child will not thrive there and deserves a more appropriate placement.

A trustee has the responsibility to support the head and to demonstrate that support within the community.

Whether the trustee has concerns about a decision that affects his own family, or a close friend, or a broader policy with which he has fundamental disagreement, the trustee should express concerns privately to head and/or chair and give public support across the board.

Specific disagreement with the head:

Gripe sessions on the golf course, check-out counter, or car-pool lines can be tempting. A trustee may want to reply, "Yeah, I don't like what she did in that case either, but…" It may help to plan a routine response on all occasions, and to simply state, "The board is aware of that situation and I am confident of a satisfactory resolution."

Similarly, the trustee may be the one who wishes to buttonhole the head with a personal concern. It can be tempting for a trustee to approach a head at the end of a long day, perhaps even at the end of a long evening board meeting, to seek special help or favor for a child. But in this case the trustee has momentarily forgotten which hat he is wearing. You attend the board meeting as a trustee, not as a parent. A wise head we know, when faced with such a request to reconsider a decision about a trustee's child at 10:30 one night, came up with a response she now uses regularly: "I know you want to speak with me as a parent, and I want to hear you out when I can give you my full attention. Tonight, you are here as a trustee and we focus on board matters. Why don't you call me first thing tomorrow and we'll find a time to talk about this family situation as soon as possible?" Successful diffusion of a potentially volatile issue is clearly important, but trustees need to be reminded of the different roles members of a school community must play at different times.

Broader disagreement with head:

A head who was consulted about one of his most promising young administrators, a candidate to head another independent school, said to the faculty and trustees of the prospective school: *"I expect you to support him when he is right — and also when he is wrong."*

As a trustee I accept my responsibility to support the head and to work through established channels to resolve differences.

There may be times when one or more trustees have a concern about what a head is doing or not doing, or how or when he or she is doing it. They may lack agreement with a new proposal the head has been testing with them. They may disagree with a variety of things. It is critically important in these cases that the trustee adheres to the school's policies and procedures. Speak directly with the head or, if you feel you can't talk with him or her, directly

❖ *What happens when I disagree with the head?*

and only with the board chair. You can expect a timely answer. In the interim, do not discuss the issue with anyone.

No head comes into the job today with all the skills and experience to lead your school. It takes time and a certain amount of trial and error. Your job as trustee is to help a head learn not to make the same mistake twice.

As a trustee, you know that your job is to help the institution see what kinds of people can help the head be most effective in every arena. As a trustee, you know that your job is to give support when right, and when wrong, even when the decision is reached that it is time for the head to leave.

❖ **What is the proper channel for complaints from constituents?**

Authority is vested in the board as a whole. A trustee who learns of an issue has the responsibility to bring it to the head of the school or the board chair and must not deal with the situation individually. Naturally members of the school community are aware of trustees' identities and will bring all manner of tales — important facts, unimportant facts, distorted facts, rumors, half-truths — to their attention. It is important that the board chair and head regularly make clear that there is only one channel of response for a trustee. "I appreciate your sharing this with me and hope you will 1) either share your concern directly with the person(s) you have named, i.e., the new seventh grade P.E. teacher, or with the appropriate administrator, division head, dean of students, etc." The trustee should also report the contact to the head of school or board chair.

Channels of communication made clear:
Unless the school has a different policy, the trustee should state clearly that the matter will only be shared by him with the head of school and/or the board chair. The head of school is preferable in most cases, but if the concern is about the head, the board chair should be the only one contacted. One of the many things head and chair should be sharing in their regular communication, as will be shown in the next chapter, is the general trend and tenor of these communications, even if there proves to be no substance to the reports.

As a trustee, you understand that no single trustee, even the chair, has any more power than another trustee, and no trustee can speak for the entire board, unless specifically authorized — e.g., "the treasurer will meet with the auditor for the purpose of authorizing the designated transfers of funds to unrestricted endowment."

The Informal Relationship

There are also many informal relationships that develop between the board members and the head, relationships that have as many variations and complexities as any other relationships. These relationships offer many opportunities: collaborating on goals and interests of priority to the school, having a good time working together to meet these goals, sharing in the joy of helping children and their teachers learn and work in a positive environment. In some cases, head and trustees will develop long-term friendships, especially if all remain aware that, as long as one person is a trustee, he or she is the other person's employer.

In the most general sense, community perceptions about some of these informal relationships may hold potential problems for the school, and for the trustees as well as the head, whether personal friendships develop or not. Anticipating some areas where problems and misunderstandings can arise can lead to strategies to avoid them.

"Getting to know you"

Heads today find they are spending more and more time getting to know each trustee as an individual, perhaps even formalizing the relationship by scheduling at least an annual one-on-one lunch.

Time-consuming as they may be, such meetings may help the head get to know the particular interests and concerns of each trustee. Heads today need and value the perspectives, experience, and talent of a variety of people in the broader world. Individual trustees can be valuable resources to a head in that regard.

When the head spends time with each trustee, the relationship allows the trustee to feel that his or her ideas are valued even if all of them may not reach the boardroom for a vote. While there are also obvious fund-raising advantages to such knowledge, there is no doubt the broader interests of the school are often well served by a strong ability to identify and tap trustee talent and interest. New trustees in particular feel welcomed to the school and to the leadership circle by such individual attention.

Some heads are now spending over a third of their time with their trustees, especially at schools in major fund-raising modes. Other members of the school community, especially faculty, may resent that the head is spending all this time with trustees, but it is time well spent on and with the people on whom the head — and the school — depend so much. And it can be fun!

In summary, the individual trustee at his or her best helps the head and the school focus on strategic issues and assures regular opportunity to evaluate and measure progress. The individual trustee understands and follows clear procedures for communication with the head. The individual trustee understands the many meanings of the responsibility of giving support to the head, especially in public, and of understanding the complexity of today's leadership challenge for heads of school.

Final thoughts

It may be instructive to reflect on the wisdom of a famous head, John Verdery of Wooster School, who was also highly sought after as a trustee by many other schools and nonprofit institutions:

> "The final and most dangerous pitfall in the process of choosing a head is to think that the wedding is the goal, when in fact it is the marriage. No new head turns out to be any more perfect than any new bride or groom. Making the marriage work takes effort on everyone's part."

Making the marriage work — keeping the head (and head's family) feeling well-supported through the good times and the bad, through successes and mistakes — this is a part of the work of every trustee.

CASE STUDIES

Letting Faculty Members Go

Dr. Juanita Robinson, a new school head, was given primary responsibility for faculty evaluation and retention by the school's board. In the middle of Dr. Robinson's second year, the school's financial situation required eliminating three faculty positions for the following year. Though the school's governance procedures did not require the head to give substantial notice to the teachers, she believed letting the teachers know as soon as possible (March, in this case) would give them time to find appropriate employment before the beginning of the next school year. Several parents, who were also trustees, were very vocal in opposing the head's actions. Three members of the executive committee met (without the chair of the board) over dinner to discuss the situation, and agreed that Dr. Robinson must review all these decisions. One trustee, the brother-in-law of one imperiled teacher, asked that the issue be placed on the agenda of the next board meeting, scheduled for April 1. Dr. Robinson met with the chair of the board to announce her plans to stick by her initial decision.

What are the issues?

What should the board do?

What should the board chair do?

What should the head do?

The Search: Inside Candidate

Valley School has entered into a search process this fall, since the current head has announced his resignation. The search committee has been charged to bring one name, its choice as the best next head of school, to the board by January if possible. A very popular and charismatic in-house administrator has applied for the position. The board doesn't want her for the job, but she is added to the finalist pool out of respect. During the fall, she wages an ambitious campaign on her own behalf with all of the school's important constituents — parents, students, alumni, and especially faculty. She even implies that there will consequences for those faculty who do not support her candidacy after she is hired! The board ignores her politicking and narrows their finalists pool to three people, including Ms. Administrator. After the finalists have been announced, one withdraws to go to another school. The board offers the head's job to the other outside candidate, who visits the school and accurately reads the brewing situation. He withdraws from the search.

What are the issues?

What should the search chair do?

What should the board do?

What should the board chair do?

What should the head do?

The Search: Split Decision

Part of the mandate given to a school's search committee is that the committee complete its search process by submitting only one name to the board for each vacancy. During the most recent search, however, the search committee is evenly split over which of two candidates, one internal and one external, to forward to the board for consideration, so they submit both names. The board will conduct a special meeting the following day to address the matter.

What are the issues?

What should the search committee do?

What should the chair do?

What should the head do?

RESOURCES

The following institutes are offered each year by the Institutional Leadership Group of NAIS. For information about dates and times, contact NAIS at (202) 973-9700, or visit the website <www.nais-schools.org>.

Leadership through Partnership (LTP). This NAIS fall workshop gives board chairs and school heads an opportunity to reflect on their own working relationship together with colleagues from other schools. Participation ranges from 60–100 schools. Annually one weekend in September or October.

Governance through Partnership (GTP). The primary goal of the NAIS Governance through Partnership Program is to develop and sustain a creative and effective governing partnership between the board and the head of school. Working with the program director and volunteer facilitators, the board and head come together at your school in a retreat or workshop setting. Held year-round on mutually agreed to dates. The program has been offered for several schools together with particular success.

Institute for New Heads (INH). The Institute for New Heads brings colleagues together at a critical early stage in their tenure as school heads to introduce key concepts and strategies of school leadership. The focus of the institute is on the head's role as intellectual, managerial, and moral leader of a complex and dynamic institution and human community. Lectures, seminars, one-on-one sessions, discussion groups with resident and visiting experts provide important perspectives on key educational issues facing schools. It is a particular goal of the institute to help heads develop personal strategies to complement their own management style as they develop an entry plan for their first months on the job. Annually for one week in July.

RESOURCES

Deal, Terrance E. and Kent D. Peterson, *The Leadership Paradox, Balancing Logic and Artistry in Schools*, Jossey-Bass, San Francisco, 1994.

Fisher, Roger and William Ury, *Getting to Yes, Negotiating Agreement Without Giving In*, Penguin Books, New York, 1991.

Fisher, James L., *The Board and the President*, American Council on Education and Macmillan, New York, 1991.

Hesselbein, Frances, Marshall Goldsmith, Richard Beckhard, Editors, *The Leader of the Future*, The Peter F. Drucker Foundation for Nonprofit Management, New York, 1996.

Houle, Cyril O., *Governing Boards, Their Nature and Nurture*, Jossey-Bass, San Francisco, 1989.

CHAPTER EIGHT

The Relationship Between the Board Chair and the Head

A true team both defines its objectives and finds ways to meet them.
— *Sally Helgensen*

As the chair of the board, you understand that there is no more important factor in the success of the school than the relationship of chair and head of school. You make central to your beliefs and actions the knowledge that together these partners share — and model — leadership and governance and determine all that follows.

As is true of the relationship between the head and all trustees, here too there are both formal and informal roles, as well as responsibilities specific to head and chair, and ones that are shared as well. It is therefore critical that the chair and head make every effort to establish a solid and mutually supportive relationship of candor and trust, develop the capacity to be mutually critical, and learn from each other's feedback — all with the goal of making their work on behalf of the school most effective.

Responsibilities of the Chair in the Board-Chair Partnership

❖ *As board chair, what are my priorities?*

◆ The chair takes the lead in areas of board leadership and management. The head takes the lead in curriculum, school operations, etc. Together they model the leadership partnership in action.

◆ The chair speaks for the board, unless someone else is delegated for a specific purpose. The chair is wise to let the head speak for the school on most occasions.

◆ The chair is the ultimate authority.

◆ The chair serves as the leader and manager of the board, and assures that:

the board does not overstep its limits,

all issues are considered, including research when necessary, and

ample time for discussion is allocated.

◆ The chair typically leads the evaluation of the head.

◆ The chair consults regularly with the head, anticipating and strategizing issues, concerns, and priorities.

◆ The chair is a ready and willing listener to the head's concerns as they emerge; he or she serves as a major advisor.

◆ The chair is a private confidante, advisor, and critic when necessary. The chair is the head's number one public advocate.

◆ The chair oversees the process of trustee selection, giving the head opportunity to review potential candidates and officers as well.

◆ The chair oversees trustee orientation.

◆ The chair organizes the board in the most effective way to conduct its business.

◆ The chair gives particular oversight and direction to the school finances and resource management.

◆ The chair needs to involve his or her successor in discussions to assure a smooth transition at the conclusion of the current chair's term. Bringing the new chair up to speed is critical to the health of the board and the school.

◆ The chair accepts the responsibility to be the disciplinarian of the board when necessary, and is willing to help counsel out unproductive, disruptive, and counterproductive trustees.

◆ The chair is willing to put in the time it takes to do all of these things. *For most NAIS member school chairs, this task averages three to four hours a week over the course of the school year.*

Responsibilities of the Head in the Board-Head Partnership

◆ The head is the executive in charge of implementing policy and goals, and oversees the daily operations of the school.

◆ The head informs and advises the chair through regular formal reports, and in a number of informal ways.

Joint Responsibilities

◆ Together the chair and head share responsibility for planning and regular review and evaluation of current plans.

◆ Together the head and chair oversee resource allocation.

◆ Together the head and chair plan board meeting agendas, executive committee work (if applicable), and assure timely evaluation of the work of the board.

◆ Together they articulate the mission and the vision of the school.

◆ They remain aware that there will be areas where lines of responsibility blur, and assure their open communication helps determine when joint presence and decision-making is most appropriate.

Cyril Houle, expert on board-CEO relations, has noted some other differences in the two positions that are instructive:

Board v. Chief executive role

The Board	The Chair	The Head
Is corporate; can act only as a group	Cannot officially act alone	Is individual
Is continuous though membership changes	Changes often in many schools	Is temporary in the life of the school
	Is part-time	Is full-time
Is part-time	Has ultimate responsibility — with full board	Has access to all staff
Has little or no staff		Has limited, immediate responsibility
Has ultimate responsibility — with chair	Typically not an expert in education	
Typically not expert in education	Volunteer	Typically is expert in education
Volunteer	Needs to be able to see big picture	Salaried
Sees only parts of the whole		Is intimately involved in everything

Acknowledging the Impact of Leadership Change and Turnover

❖ *How do we assure that the transition from one board chair to the next is a smooth one?*

Minimizing the effect of leadership change on the forward momentum of the institution, board chairs and committees on trustees need to be especially alert to the need for long-range planning for leadership succession. Who is best qualified to be the next board chair? What are his or her other commitments? Is he or she available? Who is a good alternative? Who's after that? Who will chair the capital campaign? Who will chair the committee on trustees, and when?

A school is at a critical moment every time a new chair steps on board, and current patterns of chair tenure (on average two years) often do not give the chair sufficient time to know her job and to learn all she needs to about the school. Many step down just as the learning curve begins to flatten out, leaving a new chair to start all over. A head has to learn to dance with a new partner quite often.

Heads' average tenure is now just over six years (with the median being eight). Although a number may stay at one school for fifteen-to-twenty years or even longer, many others, as much as a third of NAIS heads today, have moved on to a second or third headship. They carry a lot of cumulative experience, but in different schools. And because turnover of all members of a board, even with staggered terms of office, it is common for heads in year six or seven of a headship to find that no trustees on the current board were there when the head started the job. There is no memory of why the person was selected or of the process of determining long-range goals or shared accomplishments. There may not even be agreement with those goals. Even with a good strategic plan in place, it is hard for leaders to move the school forward with such a lack of continuity.

It is a sad fact that many of the unplanned departures of heads in recent years stem from unplanned leadership change, especially at the board chair level, which in turn has too often led to the unplanned departure of the head. These departures are inevitably disruptive to the school, as parents, teachers, and students, as well as alumni/ae and the broader world beyond the school, hold their breath and wait to see what will happen next. Anxiety goes up in the school community. Enrollment, fund-raising, and faculty, student, and parent morale may go down for a period.

The previous edition of this handbook noted in a key paragraph:

Because the head and chair are partners, the premature resignation of a head is usually a sad reflection on the performance of the board chair. They succeed or fail together. If chair and head differ too greatly in style to be able to work together, the chair should consider resigning.

There is no clearer way to make the point today.

Each independent school is different, and so is its leaders. What works for one school or pair of leaders may not be comfortable for others. But for the sake of all the constituents it is important that head and chair try to keep a consistent pattern of shared leadership to avoid sending mixed signals.

The Importance of Communication: "No Surprises"

It is to help these key school leaders learn best practices that NAIS established Leadership through Partnership, an annual workshop for heads and chairs, where the team spends two days hearing from outside experts and each other. And in the course of the weekend, they get to know each other better, too.

Each year at that workshop there is opportunity for heads to meet in small peer groups, and chairs to do the same, and reflect on certain questions put to them by one of the facilitators. One of the topics is "What is your pet peeve about your partner?" — a question designed to get troublesome issues out in the open. What is interesting is that the answers from each group tend to remain constant from year to year — and that they are not, as one might anticipate, directly complementary.

More on communication

❖ *How much do I need to share?*

Board chairs are frequently concerned that the heads do not communicate enough. This is noteworthy because heads often worry that they inundate chairs with too much information. Some heads are more deliberate about their withholding of information, but in general such a policy is apt to lead to misunderstanding or even trouble. Clearly, conversation about how much communication is desired, how often, when and where to share it will vary with the institution (boarding schools, a weekly/biweekly phone call; day schools perhaps more phone calls and even more face-to-face meetings).

A key concept for both sides is the first rule: no surprises. A chair should know about major disciplinary incidents, faculty morale, (up or down and why), a new teacher that is shaky but getting special mentoring help, staff dismissals, trustee children who are not accepted at any of their college choices or into your very own school. Obviously, more serious matters, such as a breaking news story or tragedy that might enter the media, need to be communicated immediately.

The need to know is the need to be well prepared. When in doubt, the head should pick up the phone and the chair should willingly accept the call. Most often the message requires no action from the chair, but the chair should have the information to be able to field phone calls from others and allay fears and rumors. Information sharing can also help the chair understand the pattern of daily life for the head of school.

All sharing need not be of a negative nature. A chair should get the first call, after the donor and the campaign chair, to rejoice in the news of the school's first million dollar gift, that the middle school has performed 1,000 hours of community service, that a teacher has been selected for a Klingenstein fellowship, and indeed the good news should be shared with all trustees. The board chair gets all the bad news, also, and can help strategize the head's response, if needed.

Disciplining Trustees: A Job for the Chair

❖ *Why is this my job as chair?*

The heads' pet peeve about their board chairs is a very specific one: "I have a chair who won't discipline the maverick or renegade trustee," i.e., the one who has gone way beyond the established procedure and is stirring up trouble with inappropriate communication to other members of the board and the community. Most often this is the trustee with a particular agenda, someone who is unwilling to work within established parameters.

The trustee behaving inappropriately can be very damaging to the school, particularly if allowed to continue unchecked. While in extreme cases the chair may have to ask for a resignation, or even take steps to remove a reluctant trustee, a candid conversation will often change the tactics the trustee is using. The conversation is one for the chair to have, not the head.

It can be hard. "How can I discipline a volunteer? They give their time, their money." "I didn't agree to do this when I signed up to be chair. Let's just let him ride out his term." "Maybe we can give her part of what she wants."

No. The chair must intervene firmly.

Metaphors of Teamwork for Head and Chair

Many images have been used by students of governance for this partnership team of head and chair, and naturally many of these images derive from the world of sports where teamwork is so important and so consciously worked on every day.

Let's look at three examples: a three-legged race; a tennis doubles partnership; and the pitcher-catcher analogy from baseball. Each of these glimpses has something to offer a head and chair embarking on a new relationship, or a continuing one.

❖ *Tell me about teamwork between head and chair.*

A three-legged race

To perform well in this race, the partners must agree on the pace they will set, who will stride forward with which lead, and in which direction will they go. If they are not in agreement, one will fall and they will both be set back.

Tennis doubles

The metaphor makes clear that the older metaphor of tennis singles — chair tackling all policy issues on one side of a clearly defined barrier, and head tackling all management issues on the other side — was inadequate. Although there are clear lines between the role of the board and the chair, and the role of the administration and the head, it is never so clear as to have everything on one side of the net be the board's business, and, on the other, the head's. Too many decisions require the best joint thinking, strategy, and action. Sometimes circumstances necessitate shared action. In doubles, one player may play several shots in a row, run back to the baseline, then up to the net, even crossing over, briefly, into the other partner's space and then quickly return to the spot where they play most of their game.

There may be decisions and actions in a school about which a head would normally take the lead, where, for reasons of local culture and circumstance, a chair may be the better person to do so. The central agreement must be one to respect each other's basic responsibilities. A parallel agreement is to not let formal structure override, in specific instances, common sense. As in tennis doubles, the partners who play together for a time and are willing to critique each other's games and anticipate and reduce points of friction, are the ones who learn from experience and become a winning team.

Catcher-pitcher relationship

Yogi Berra, the famous New York Yankee catcher, once noted in *The New York Times* the important, but largely secondary role in the eyes of spectators, that a catcher plays in a pitcher's performance. "Pitchers," he wrote in a tone in which some board chairs may find familiar, "think they know everything." Obviously neither pitchers nor heads of school know everything, even if mostly they are the experts on what is happening. The role of the catcher is to help suggest strategies; what to do when, and how to do it. And just as a pitcher can shake off a catcher's suggestion for certain pitches, so can a head choose to "call the pitches." However, the wise head takes in and responds to good counsel from a good board chair.

Berra also said, a further responsibility of the catcher is to "know which guys to yell at and which you have to just pet." Of course we are not recommending a board chair either yell at or directly pet a head of school, but metaphorically there are times the chair must take the lead in encouraging, or discouraging, a head from continuing on the present course. The head, as pitcher, is largely the leader on camera, out on center stage each day. The chair, like the catcher, can help make the team more effective by serving as ongoing strategist and coach. The chair can, metaphorically, interrupt the game occasionally to walk out to the mound and exchange a few words, to help calm a pitcher who may have made two or three bad pitches in a row, or to schedule a longer talk in the middle of a losing streak. How effectively the catcher does this can determine a winning or losing game, and season. The same with the best board chairs.

As the board chair, you accept the role of coach, confidant, strategist, friendly critic, and number one supporter of the head.

Chair as Official Nurturer of the Head

❖ *The head knows I care. Why do I have to tell her?*

In addition to the chair's official responsibilities to share information with a head, he or she is also a major sustainer of a head's health and morale, even if the head has a supportive circle of family and friends. There are many ways to do this: a pair of tickets to the symphony, the offer of a beach house for the weekend, the suggestion or insistence that the head stay out of the office two weeks at a time over the winter and spring breaks and for a full month in the summer, etc. Board chairs should also be aware that heads have lives outside of school and that immediate family issues may take precedence over school issues at certain times. Acknowledgment of the need for a support network for the head, who too often can be assumed to be willing to give 100 percent of her life to the school, is vital. These are real issues, and come with the territory of board chair's nurturing, caring role with the head.

Chair as Communicator of a Serious Message

❖ *How do we handle bad news?*

In addition to the many kinds of information sharing where the head passes on bad news to the board chair for information only, the board chair may from time to time have bad news to share with the head that is substantive and significant. It may be about something the head has done, or not done, that has not been well received by some person or part of the school community. If it's important, the information must be shared with the head as soon as possible. Don't wait for an annual evaluation report.

This is not the kind of conversation to be had on the run or in a phone call. It deserves time and space of its own. The head needs time to reply, immediately and perhaps more formally several days later. The head may need to find more information, to help distinguish between fact or rumor. The perceived error or errors may be ones of omission, or of commission.

After sharing the concern and hearing the head's response, the chair and head then strategize together to make sure that there is a plan to resolve the present issue and to minimize recurrence of whatever was the matter. In most cases, the problem can be resolved and, with the chair's visible support, the school and the partnership can continue to move forward.

If in time, the rarer situation occurs when a series of such conversations indicate to the head the sense of the entire board that it is time for the school to seek a new head for the year after next, the special job of the board chair in that final year is to assure that the head can leave with a sense of clarity and completion.

The essential elements in all this communication are trust, respect, and a willingness to work to make the relationship better in order to help the school become more effective.

As a board chair you accept the responsibility of working with the head to resolve differences and problems throughout the head's tenure. As board chair you understand the importance of direct, mutually established goals to the head's annual evaluation and to the board's evaluation and your own as well. As board chair you understand that in accepting the leadership of the board, you make a serious commitment of mind and heart to the school and the head. You will work hard with your partner and share and enjoy the challenge.

CASE STUDIES

New Head, New Methods

Thomas Stephens, an experienced head of school, leaves a successful headship after eight years in a K–8 country day school and takes a new position as head of a K–12 day school in another state. His experience as a skillful leader in his previous school and as a trustee of his state association of independent schools were clear factors in his appointment. He is nationally known for his close work with his several board chairs in effective implementation of new models for board organization, particularly in reducing and streamlining board committees and increasing the number of specific ad hoc task forces to create meaningful and productive work for the board.

At the new school he and the board chair begin a process of moving in this direction with the new board. Together they create two task forces, one focusing on technology and one on diversity issues and at the same time suspend the previous practice of having each committee report at each board meeting.

In late fall the board chair is called unexpectedly to a new city and a job assignment, and the vice chair takes over as board chair. The new chair is an alumna of the school, class of 1957, and learned her trusteeship in the traditional model, where board committees parallel the internal organization of the school (education, buildings and grounds, finance, etc.) and is comfortable with that model. She believes "if it ain't broke, don't fix it," and says she has heard from several trustees that they miss the opportunity to report on the work of their committees at each meeting. In her regular meeting with the head in early February, she tells the head she has agreed to disband the task forces and return to the previous way of board organization.

This is the first the head has heard of this turn-around.

What are the issues?

What should the head do?

What should the board do?

What should the chair do?

Micromanaging the Curriculum

The chair of the education committee and the chair of the board (without input from the head) have agreed to review the reading curriculum's Phonics vs. Whole Language approaches and set up a process to interview teachers and parents and to monitor and observe classes. One day, the head receives a phone call from Andreas Likurgos, a first-grade reading teacher, who wonders "why trustee Smith is sitting in my room." The head calls the chair of the board (who has children at the school in grades K and 2) to find out what is going on. The chair claims that the goal of the program is impartial fact gathering "without the involvement of the head and without giving faculty time for special preparation for the observation periods." The education committee wanted to see the reading curriculum "like it really was" implemented in the classroom.

What are the issues?

What should the head do?

What should the chair do?

What should the board do?

CHAPTER NINE

Relating to Major Constituencies or Stakeholders

The only definition of a leader is someone who has followers.

— *Peter Drucker*

As a trustee, you are a guardian of the school's human, financial, and physical resources, working to assure that they are sufficient to accomplish the school's goals and plans and are well managed. Your fellow trustees, the head, administrators, faculty, parents, alumnae/i, students, funders, and friends all are major stakeholders of the school. You celebrate the diversity of the school's supporters and the diversity within those supporters.

Multiplicity of Relationships

You interact with all of these stakeholders in formal, planned ways, such as at meetings and events, and informally, such as in the parking lot or walking across campus. Each of these relationships is different. Each brings its own set of rewards and potential problems. If the school is fulfilling its mission with vision and energy, the school's constituents will be bound together by this mission.

Trustees need to be clear about how to manage both their formal and informal contacts because a lack of clarity around these interactions can lead to negative situations. With faculty, administrators, and other staff you are the ultimate "boss" because you, as a board member, hire and evaluate the head, who in turn is the school's CEO and staff leader. You may be a parent or an alumnus/a, yet you are part of board decisions that constituency may not like. With students you may be seen as the mother or father of one of their friends or you may be off their radar screen all together. If students do know about trustees and their role, you may be seen as just one more authority figure, making decisions that affect their lives for good or ill. With funders and friends from the community you may share a great deal, such as living in the same neighborhood or working in the same building or you may have barely or never met them. You, as a trustee, must keep them in mind as you make decisions because the success of the school may depend on their generosity with their resources — money, time, and expertise. However, you never let funders drive your decisions. If you think that your board member role can complicate your school relationships, you are right!

The trustee/head relationship, which is the most critical relationship of all, shapes the board's view of its interactions with administrators and faculty members. After the head, board members find themselves most often with administrators and faculty members. The head is the "gatekeeper" of the interaction between the trustees and the staff. She/he works with administrators and the chair to establish the parameters of the relationships and then shares the "rules" with all involved, trustees and staff alike. This does not mean that the board and staff cannot meet and enjoy each other's company. It does mean that there is a clear understanding of the communication chain, and that the head is the point person for administrators and teachers.

Interacting with Administrators and Faculty

While not every school is able to afford a full complement of administrators, this discussion presupposes that there are paid professionals for most major functions. It should always be remembered that the trustees, head, and administrators exist to enable the faculty to fulfill the school's mission of providing an excellent education for its students.

Formal opportunities to interact

Most trustees work with administrators and faculty members while serving on committees/ task forces. Business managers, development directors, admission

directors, academic division heads or deans, and teachers with special skills
or interest in serving on committees are the individuals with whom board
members interact most. Administrators often attend board meetings at least
for part of the time, though not at every meeting, and may give updates on
activities over which they have supervision.

Informal opportunities to interact

Social and sporting events are among the most frequent places trustees meet
administrators and teachers. At day schools, trustees, especially those who
are parents, run into staff members all the time around the school. Boarding
school trustees have fewer opportunities to interact with teachers and administrators, but many such schools schedule social gatherings when trustees are
on campus for their meetings.

Rewards

Administrators and faculty members bring their expertise to planning and
policy development. They are grounded in the day-to-day demands and work
of the school and so can offer advice that is a valuable reality check to the
board's deliberations. At the same time they can visualize and articulate an
exciting future for the school. They are colleagues of trustees as they all plan
for and support the school and its students.

Potential problems

❖ *I just never
could stand
Johnny's
third-grade
teacher and
he's still
here!*

Individual trustees and staff or faculty can forge alliances to circumvent the
head and board chair and established procedures. Usually this happens over a
grievance or the desire to further a personal agenda. As a trustee, do not get
drawn into a subversion of policies or procedures or an "end-run" around the
head or chair. If you are not sure if policies or procedures, such as a grievance
structure or communications plan, are in place, find out. If they do not exist,
work with trustees and/or staff to develop them, and where appropriate, bring
them to the board for approval. Tell the head or chair of any approaches to
you by teachers or administrators that circumvent the established rules. Also,
the head should counsel her/his staff to do the same if a trustee contacts
them improperly.

Faculty members can have special relationships with trustees who are
current or past parents because they have taught or are teaching the trustee's

children. Children and their teachers can have very positive or very negative interactions — or both over the course of a year. This experience can color the parents' relationship with the teachers and then can carry over to board members' attitudes about individual teachers and the faculty as a whole. Parent-trustees, when advocating for their children with administrators or teachers, need to take off their trustee hat. Remember, it is hard for faculty to view trustee-parents without that hat. Board members need to be focused on the well-being of the total staff and also to work collegially with individual members in their committee/task force endeavors. Never use your position as a trustee to put added pressure on a faculty member, or use your trustee position to gain unfair advantage for your child. In fact, good trustees often bend over backwards the other way.

Interacting with Parents

One of the most sensitive relationships for trustees is that with parents, especially when the trustee is also a parent of a child in the school.

Formal opportunities to interact

❖ *You want me to tell the head that?*

Board committee meetings find many parents and trustees working together. Non-trustee parents often serve on board committees, especially the development, buildings and grounds, and finance committees. Development and fund-raising activities also mix trustees, parents, and alumnae/i together, whether it be annual and capital campaigns or special events. Schools may have policies that non-trustee parents may not serve on certain committees, which can include the education, personnel, and financial aid committees because their agendas involve faculty and staff and the program. Some schools do not want parents serving on the committee on trustees because of the confidential nature of its work.

The parents association (also known as the parents' organization, the parents/teachers association, and the parents/teachers organization) is the school organization that works to welcome parents and their children to the school, plans and implements parent nights and other parent forums, and raises funds, in concert with the school's development plan. The chair of the association, or another representative, may serve on the board of trustees as an ex-officio member. (Remember, ex-officio members have a vote, unless

148

the bylaws state that they serve "ex-officio, without a vote.") It is very important for the board of trustees to keep the association leadership informed of the board's major decisions so that parent leaders can be prepared for questions from the parent-body. If there is no formal personal liaison on the board, a system for informing association leaders should be established.

Informal opportunities to interact

Day school board members have incredible opportunities to be with parents on and off school grounds — parking lots, parties, athletic events, grocery stores, fund raisers, etc. Boarding schools may have the same opportunities if they also have a large number of day students. Otherwise, their trustees interact infrequently with the parent body, and when they do, it most often is at planned events.

Respecting parents

❖ *We couldn't do anything major without the support of the parents!*

Parents have made a major step in supporting the school's mission. They have entrusted their child to the school for her or his education. They have expended a considerable amount of their financial assets to pay the tuition. They care deeply about the success of the school because its success benefits their child. In spite of the fact that many of today's parents work outside the home, they volunteer in great numbers for almost every aspect of the school, and they often are generous donors to the annual and capital campaigns. Parents expect and deserve great consideration in deliberations of the board.

Potential problems

Parents are very close to the school's program. They are consumers of what the school offers, and, as such they question and question and question. This is not bad in and of itself, but it does become a problem when parents substitute their opinions for those of the experts hired to educate their children — the teachers. Many heads can tell stories of parents who constantly complain and then, when it is suggested that they might be happier at another school, become outraged. Parent-trustees who continually base their governance decisions on their personal experiences with their own children should be counseled off the board by the chair.

Trustees must not allow themselves to be drawn into the problems of a school family. They need to listen politely, to tell the parents that trustees do not have any authority over their situation, ask them to talk to the appropriate administrator or the head, and then tell the head immediately about the conversation.

Interacting with Alumnae/i

❖ *What do you mean the school is going to change the color of the shutters?*

Alumnae/i can play critical roles on the campus. They are found among parents, funders, and trustees, and they are living examples of the education provided by the school.

Formal opportunities to interact

Alumnae/i serve as trustees and often are involved in fund development activities, including leadership roles. Schools have established career development programs where alumnae/i offer presentations to the students and mentor students who are interested in the alumnae/i's fields of interest. They even give advice and open up job possibilities to fellow graduates across the country. They host cultivation/fund-raising social events for alumnae/i living in areas far from the school. Most schools have alumnae/i associations which are the vehicles for graduates to express their opinions and to raise funds, in coordination with the school's development plan. Often, the chair of the association or another representative, serves ex-officio on the board of trustees and, in that capacity, the association chair/representative can bring alumnae/i issues to the attention of the board and board decisions back to the association. Elementary schools are increasingly forming alumnae/i associations, as they reach out to encourage their graduates to provide the financial and other support they have traditionally given to their secondary schools.

Informal opportunities to interact

Day schools will have more of their graduates in the "neighborhood" than boarding schools. However, with today's mobile society, alumnae/i of day schools live all over the country. Trustees can meet graduates anywhere and everywhere, just as they do parents, and it is an added joy for schools to have a good number of alumnae/i parents in the school because it is the ultimate endorsement.

Rewards

One hopes that graduates will be the best advertisement for the school wherever they find themselves. If they are kept well informed, alumnae/i can be enthusiastic and productive fund-raisers, since they already have a deep commitment to the school. Often this attachment to the school is demonstrated in their relationships with other graduates and current students in the area of career planning and assistance in finding jobs. They can be among the most valuable volunteers for the school no matter where they live.

Potential problems

Graduates who are disaffected and vocal can be very damaging to a school's reputation. Whether it is a distrust of current practices or unhappiness with their own student experiences, they can cause people to question placing their own children in the school. When serving on the board of trustees or its committees, some alumnae/i have trouble with changes at the school since their graduation and thus balk at needed innovations; they perceive themselves as the keepers of tradition. Graduates such as these see the school as "their" school, not as their school and the school for current and future students. This is not to say that traditions are bad; they are very important in the life of any school. They facilitate community building and a sense of connectedness to the past. Most current students are curious about the history of their school, especially about the students that proceeded them. The concern is that tradition not be a barrier to the future. Rather it should unify and be an opportunity for celebration.

Interacting with Students

❖ *So that's why we're here!*

The *students* are the reason for the school's existence — the reason that there are trustees, heads, faculty, and staff. They are why funds are raised, buildings are painted, plans are promulgated, committees meet, and on and on.

Formal opportunities to interact

Some boards of trustees include students on committees/task forces and hold dinners with student leaders or even the whole student body. It is hoped that trustees will attend sports events, plays, art exhibits, student debates, etc. in order to demonstrate their support of the students and see them in action.

This can be difficult for boarding schools, but many schedule student events during trustee weekend meetings on campus.

Informal opportunities to interact

These are more difficult to accomplish, as students are busy in school — or they should be! However, trustees can have conversations with students when they attend campus events. Today's students are not shy about sharing their opinions, concerns, and joys. Of course, parent-trustees have a myriad of occasions when they can interact with students, including driving carpools and sitting around the kitchen table.

Rewards

Students bring an immediacy to issues because they are one part of the equation that constitutes the education provided at the school. Just as faculty and parents have their opinions about how the school should implement its program, so do students. Trustees need to value their ideas and check-in in appropriate ways to assess how the students feel about their school life. It should not be forgotten that they are children, but children can often be just as on-target as adults can. Age alone does not guarantee wisdom.

Potential problems

Trustees need to be sure that they do not become involved with a particular student's problem, whether it concerns academics or behavior. Students are not perfect; they do get in trouble — even model students. Fortunately, they don't usually ask their parents (or another adult connected with the school) to intervene on their behalf. The problems arise when a concerned parent or friend's parent is a trustee who cannot separate the parent role from that of trustee.

❖ *Some of the best support can come from outside the immediate community.*

Interacting with Funders and Friends

Funders and friends from beyond the immediate school community are valuable not only for their financial contributions, but also for their connections and advice. Corporate foundations seldom fund independent schools, unless they match employees' gifts, while private independent and family foundations can be very generous benefactors. Friends of the school may be educators from all areas and levels of education, community leaders, neighbors of the school, vendors, etc. They feel connected to the school, but not as directly as the constituents mentioned above. Thus, trustees and others associated with the school need to realize that anywhere they find themselves, they are identified as representing the school. They have the opportunity and obligation to advocate for the school — its mission, program, and students.

Formal opportunities to interact

Funders may be invited to events honoring their gifts, school sponsored educational programs, scheduled visits to the school to see what their gifts have enabled, etc. Wherever it is appropriate and does not take away from the primacy of the students, their program, or needs, members of the community-at-large should be welcomed to attend educational programs, visual and performing art shows, and the like. This is "friend raising" at its broadest and best.

Informal opportunities to interact

As was noted, you may not know that you are in the presence of funders and friends, and, as a trustee, you need to be prepared to advocate for the school at any moment and in any place you find yourself.

Rewards

"Outsiders," funders and friends alike, can bring new perspectives, financial support, and wisdom to the school. They can expand the school's reach to more diverse populations and become allies in promoting the school to their own friends.

Potential problems

Funders can offer resources with conditions which could cause the school to alter its mission if they accepted these resources. If a school adopts such practices, over time the school may or may not be solvent, but it will have lost its integrity, and its board members will have abdicated their moral trusteeship.

Working with Educational Associations

Many schools are involved with local, state, regional, and national independent school associations, as well as organizations devoted to specific sectors of the independent school community, such as those for boarding schools, girls' schools, religiously affiliated schools, etc. Trustees need to be aware of and support these relationships through encouraging administrators and faculty members to participate in the associations and organizations. Trustees, themselves, may also play a role, in a way that the members of NAIS's Trustee Advisory Committee do. Independent schools can have very positive, rather than competitive, relationships with public school systems and individual public schools. Such partnerships frequently strengthen both public and private institutions, for both have much to give to and learn from each other.

As a trustee, you work to keep the diverse stakeholders of the school connected to each other and to keep their interests and needs in your thoughts during board deliberations, while making decisions in the best interest of the school as a whole. You relish the diversity of perspectives, talents, and backgrounds of the school community, especially nurturing the strengths and potential of each and every student. You are the guardian of their well-being and that of generations of students to come. You hold the school's future in your hands.

CASE STUDY

The Pick of the Crop?

Pippin School, in the California farming town of Appleborough, has for sixty-five years served as the region's only independent school option. A K–8 school, it accepts nearly all applicants, except for those with significant learning differences. Its families reflect a range of socioeconomic backgrounds, from small-town business owners and professionals to working farm families. Graduates attend local public schools for the most part, though a few venture to more distant independent high schools.

In recent years, Appleborough has become something of a bedroom community for Big Orchard sixty miles away, due to suburbanization and improved highways, which have brought many more prosperous families to the old farms and ranches. Over the past three or four years, new parents, including some recently appointed to the board, have pointed with alarm to the fact that school test scores consistently fall below the national independent school averages. Demands for "academic excellence" and greater challenge have come from those parents whose children score high, or whose ambitions for their children include attendance at the most selective colleges.

At the traditional open board meetings in June, several parents accuse the board of shirking its responsibility to oversee the educational program, and demand that higher academic standards be adopted throughout the school for the coming year. Two board members announce their complete agreement with these parents, and the meeting ends in a mood of distress and unhappiness.

What are the issues?

What should the board do?

What should the chair of the board do?

What should the head do?

RESOURCES

Ellis, Susan J., *The Board's Role in Effective Volunteer Involvement*, National Center for Nonprofit Boards, Washington, DC, 1995.

Leadership Forum, National Assocation of Independent Schools, Washington, DC (NAIS membership biannual newsletter).

Head's Letter, Educational Directions, Inc., Providence, RI (newsletter).

Trustee's Letter, Educational Directions, Inc., Providence, RI (newsletter).

CHAPTER TEN

Organizing an Effective Board

I look carefully at how a workplace organizes [itself], not its tasks, functions, and hierarchies, but the patterns and relationships and capacities available to form them.

— *Margaret J. Wheatley*

As a trustee, you are part of a diverse and complicated school community. You work to assure that the board is effective and focused on its work of fulfilling the mission and bettering the well-being of that community. You do not "run" the school; you govern through planning, monitoring, and evaluating. You add value to the board's life and to the school.

Underlying Organizational Principles

Every board of trustees has a fundamental responsibility for self-management by creating a structure, policies, and procedures that support good governance. There is not a "one size fits all" board structure that you can pull off the shelf and adopt. There are a number of approaches to organizational format, but whichever one meets your board's current and future needs, it should demonstrate the following to be effective:

◆ Is economical, simple, and as efficient as collective decision-making can be.

◆ Keeps board work at the policy, institutional level and not at the operational level. (The old adage, "nose in, fingers out" or "NIFO," applies here.)

◆ Delineates responsibilities and requires accountability.

◆ Maintains an orderly flow of work from committees or task groups to the board.

◆ Establishes ongoing evaluation and monitoring procedures.

◆ Facilitates the involvement of all trustees in major board decisions.

◆ Encourages open communications within the board and among the board and the school's constituencies.

◆ Allows for ongoing training and education of trustees.

◆ Provides efficient, effective use of trustees' time.

Boards need to consider board structural issues carefully: board size, board meeting frequency, length, and agenda, board retreats, committee structure, and whether to have committees or not, etc. After the selection of trustees, the manner in which the board governs is the key to its effectiveness. The majority of NAIS member schools have traditional board structures with committees that closely parallel the operational functions of the school: finance, development, buildings and grounds, education, personnel, student life, and financial aid — but more alternative structures appear every year.

Two other committees under this structure are governance committees: the committee on trustees and executive committee. There can be other committees, either standing (ongoing) or ad hoc (time-limited), such as strategic planning and capital campaign committees. Another type of governance framework stresses the shared work of board and staff around critical school issues. The resulting structure, often task forces with clear mandates and clear starting and ending points, involves fewer formal committees and more issue and time specific work groups. A third approach is called "policy governance" which emphasizes the importance of boards working as a whole on policy issues that define the vision, set desired end results, establish the parameters within which the staff operates, and monitor results and observance of the boundaries (see p. 165 for more on alternative governance structures).

This chapter is devoted mainly to the traditional committee structure and the possibility of combining some of these committees to streamline the board structure. The other systems will be described briefly. The chapter's resource section contains information on the work of two pioneers in this field, John Carver and Richard Chait.

Traditional Committee Structure

❖ *Why all these committee meetings?*

The traditional committee structure continues in place at schools for the most part because it accomplishes the work of the board. The question trustees need to ask is, "Is this the most efficient and effective manner to organize ourselves?" The answer may be "yes" or "maybe" or "no." One way to get the most accurate response is to pretend there was no structure to the board and then delineate the functions for which the board is responsible. Then build a committee structure to meet these responsibilities, check the new structure against the current one and the underlying principles found in this chapter, and adapt the original structure, if necessary.

The following committee descriptions are brief and not meant to be definitive. Committee and task groups need clear, concise job descriptions and yearly plans that further the school's strategic plan. See the resource section at the end of this chapter for information on committee job descriptions. Remember that not all schools will have all these committees; it's a matter of need and choice.

Finance committee

In concert with staff, this committee develops the long-range financial plan and yearly operational budget, with tuition levels for board approval; monitors the implementation of the budget; makes periodic reports to the board on the school's financial status; and educates the board on nonprofit financial reporting and trends affecting the school's finances. (For more information on the board's role in assuring the school's financial well-being, see Chapter 5.) This committee can include outside experts on finances and financial planning as members.

Investment committee

This can be a subcommittee of the finance committee. It develops and recommends to the board for its approval policies that delineate how the school's endowment will be invested and what amount of return on investment will be used in the yearly operating budget; monitors the investment portfolio's return, including setting investment objectives and meeting with the professional advisor; and periodically reports to the board on the endowment's performance. Some investment committees actually manage endowment funds, but this practice is not recommended because of the objective expertise and time necessary to do a truly effective job. (See Chapter 5.)

Audit committee

This committee should be independent of the finance committee because the audit function can include an evaluation of how the finance committee performs its oversight of the school's resources. It recommends the independent auditor for board approval; works with the auditor to establish the scope of the audit; reviews the recommendations for improvement of internal controls found in the auditor's management letter; recommends approval of the annual audit to the board; and monitors the implementation of the recommendations of the management letter. (See Chapter 5.)

Building and grounds committee

This committee develops the master plan of the school's buildings and grounds with the staff and outside consultants, if employed, for board approval; monitors implementation of the plan; reports to the board periodically on major plant and campus issues; keeps the finance committee informed on buildings and grounds needs. This can be the committee that provides board oversight of major building projects, but does not act as the project manager. (A special board committee can be constituted to oversee the project for its duration). The buildings and grounds committee does not get involved in day-to-day operations, such as roof leaks, maintenance of playing fields, selection of carpeting, etc., but it should be especially attentive to the deferred maintenance needs of the plant. It can include parents or others with expertise in construction and allied fields and students as members.

Personnel committee

In cooperation with the head, this committee develops broad personnel policies, such as benefits offered, salary ranges, and the requirement for faculty and staff evaluation. It recommends to the board, through the budget process, salary pool increases. It does not get involved in implementing the policies, such as setting individual salaries, or evaluating staff.

Financial aid committee

Works with staff to develop policies concerning the eligibility and administration of aid; recommends policies to the board; and recommends, through the budget process, the percentage of the budget dedicated to financial aid. It does not decide who will get aid or how much aid will be given to a student.

Education committee

This committee concentrates on issues at the broadest level; develops and recommends to the board educational policies, such as the type of education offered at the school (college prep, arts, vocational, elementary, high school, etc.); assesses the overall school performance against the strategic plan; can play a major role when the school is in the accreditation process; and reports periodically to the board. This committee does not set the curriculum or evaluate teachers. Committee members can include school faculty and administrators and outside educators.

NOTE: Trustees who are members of the education committee often find such service frustrating, as the curriculum is the responsibility of the head and faculty, and it is not clear what their role is. In fact, a number of boards have decided against having such a committee and instead have handled major educational issues through the strategic planning process.

Student life committee

This committee concerns itself with broad policy issues beyond academic area, such as the breadth of extracurricular and sports programs and the building of community, and works with the head to develop and implement opportunities for trustees to interact. It does not plan specific student activities, such as which sports will be offered. Students make excellent committee members, as their perspective can be very helpful.

Development committee

This committee coordinates the fund-raising activities of the school; advises the board on the financial goals of the annual campaign, through the budget process, and on any capital or endowment campaign; reviews the case statement for any fund appeal; facilitates the inclusion of all trustees and other volunteers in fund- and friend-raising activities; and raises funds. This committee should not be viewed as the only group that brings in financial resources to the school; trustees, parents and alumnae/i all should be involved in ways that are appropriate for them. Of course, everyone on the committee should be a donor before soliciting funds from others. (See Chapter 5 for more information on the board's role in assuring the financial strength of the school.)

Strategic planning committee

In concert with the head, faculty, and administrators, this committee develops the strategic plan, with its mission statement, goals, and strategic issues, for board approval and can monitor the plan's implementation. Often, the committee is limited in time because the implementation monitoring is assigned to the executive committee and/or other committees whose charge touches on specific sections of the plan. The development of action plans is the responsibility of the head, unless the goal concerns governance issues. The committee can include non-trustee parents and outside experts. (See Chapter 6 for more information.)

Committee on trustees

This committee coordinates the identification, cultivation, recruitment, and orientation of new trustees; renominates sitting trustees; nominates officers; facilitates board self-assessment; identifies board's needs for education and training and designs vehicles to meet the needs; and organizes the recognition of individual trustees. At some schools the committee nominates members of the committee on trustees. All nominations are sent to the board for its approval. (See Chapter 6 for more information.)

Executive committee

This committee coordinates, with the board chair, the work of the board; serves as a sounding board for the head; acts in place of the board between board meetings in the manner prescribed by the bylaws and as expressly delegated by the board; and reports any actions to the board in a timely fashion. This is not a super-board; it does not make policy.

If the executive committee takes over the board's role, the board will either become passive and uninvolved or angry. Neither reaction leads to effective governance of the school. Some schools do not want an executive committee in order to avoid the dangers described above, but most find that the committee can be helpful in expediting the board's business. Boarding schools may use executive committees as a means to keep a core of board members involved because the full board tends to meet only three to four times a year. Thus, these committee members need to be especially vigilant to assure that the board is the governing body of the school, not the executive committee.

The bylaws usually state who should serve on the committee. Most often it is the officers and chairs of the major standing committees. Some executive committees have members-at-large, appointed by the chair.

Head's advisory committee

This committee, whose members are selected by the head, serves to counsel the head on her or his concerns with individuals or constituent groups. It can be of assistance when differences arise between the head and trustees, including the chair. The committee usually consists of two to three members and does not include the chair. Several major problems can arise if this committee becomes the gatekeeper for trustee access to the head, is confused with the executive committee, or stands in the way of what should be a close relationship between the head and board chair. This committee is not found on most boards, but some schools have used it only during the new head's first year in order to support her/his entry into the new school community. It is often called the transition committee and may include special support for the head's family in their new community.

Combining Traditional Committees

In an effort to streamline their operations, some boards have grouped traditional committees into larger functional committees. These larger committees may or may not have subcommittees that split up tasks. The following is just one attempt at this grouping:

◆ Resource/Asset Management
    Finance
    Buildings and Grounds
    Investment
    Personnel

◆ Institutional Advancement
    Development (including public relations)
    Capital/Endowment Campaign
    Relate to: Alumnae/i Association
                 Parents Association

◆ School Life
    Education
    Student Life

Committee Assignments

❖ *How did
I end up
on this
committee?*

A school's bylaws normally give the board chair the authority to appoint committee chairs. With committee chairs in place, committee membership is then generally selected in one of two ways:

◆ The board chair appoints committee members, usually in consultation with the committee chairs and head of school.

◆ The committee chairs choose the members of their committees, usually in consultation with the board chair and head of school.

Many schools ask their trustees to indicate their committee preference in ranked order of interest. The committee on trustees, acting in its board development role, may recommend specific trustee committee assignments to the board chair for members being groomed for leadership positions. The idea is to move trustees beyond their areas of expertise to a broader knowledge of the work of the entire board. This experience will make them better board leaders when their time comes.

Alternative Board Structures

There is a great deal of academic research and practical experimentation with a variety of governance structures. The following are brief descriptions of the works of two of the leaders in this field, Richard Chait and John Carver. For information on some of their work see the resource section at the end of this chapter.

Chait, along with his colleagues Barbara E. Taylor and Thomas P. Holland, has studied nonprofit boards and has come to the conclusion that effective governance is rare. He posits that boards and management must work together to determine the critical issues of their organization and to keep the agenda going forward. Both trustees and the CEO (head) need to understand what matters to the organization's stakeholders, and this means that trustees need to have in-depth interactions with their constituents. They also need to enlist the advice of experts, some of whom may be on the board and many of whom will not. After learning what really matters, the board and CEO work collaboratively to develop and implement policy and then monitor its effectiveness with predetermined measurements.

This style of interaction fuses the traditional lines of policy development and implementation. The board structure is issue-based, ad hoc, and flexible. Board meetings are organized around issues and allow for in-depth discussions and thoughtful decisions. Meeting agendas change from meeting to meeting, and the board becomes energized because it is clear that every trustee's input is valued and the board's collective wisdom makes a difference in the school. Thus an effective board is a "constellation," not a collection of "stars."

Carver also stresses the collective nature of effective boards. He has coined the phrase "policy governance" to describe a board that develops four categories of policies:

◆ *Ends:* define who is to be served and how, in terms of the long-range vision of the organization, and is mission related.

◆ *Executive Limits:* set forth the limits within which the staff operates and leaves all within the boundaries up to staff for decisions and implementation.

◆ *Board-Staff Linkages:* delineates how the board delegates authority and evaluates staff performance on the achievement of ends and observation ofexecutive limits policies.

◆ *Governance Process:* prescribes how the board will perform its own work, which should include the establishment of policies, the evaluation of CEO (head's) performance, and maintenance of connections to its stakeholders.

This form of governance calls for the board to act as a whole, sets forth very few board committees, and focuses on long-range issues/concerns.

Board Size

❖ *What is the perfect number of trustees?*

One of the governance questions most asked of NAIS is, "What should the size of the board be?" There is no perfect size. The average number of trustees on NAIS member schools' boards is 21, but that really is not a guide to the "right" number for your school. The ideal number of board members is the smallest number of trustees that allows your board to be effective. The size of the school, whether it is a day or boarding school, the range of grades, all can influence the size of the board. However, the board's organizational structure is the key factor in board size. If there is a multiplicity of committees (even with a large number of non-trustees on its committees), the board will need to be larger than one that has fewer committees or focuses on "policy governance." A board is too large when the chair has to spend an inordinate amount managing the work of the board, rather than leading the board, and when staff must devote their scarce time to generating mounds of paper, assisting at a multitude of meetings, etc.

Successful board meetings

❖ *Why can't we ever get a quorum?*

No matter how a board is organized, board meetings need to focus on issues that further the school's mission and vision; evaluate current policies; and assess the performance of the school, head, and the board itself. Meetings should not end up as events where intelligent, talented, and thoughtful people gather to approve minutes and listen to reports that just as easily could have been mailed in advance of the meeting.

What are the ingredients of successful board meetings? They should:

◆ inform, educate, or inspire trustees

◆ make good use of the assembled expertise to benefit the school

◆ involve examining strategic directions through in-depth discussion

◆ identify and resolve conflict

◆ reach conclusions, whether by a formal vote or consensus

Board agendas should be developed by the board chair, in consultation with the head, and, once at the meeting, the agenda belongs to the board as a whole and the chair only facilitates discussion. Time should be reserved for board development — education and training. It seems only appropriate for trustees of educational institutions to value education for themselves. Every meeting should have a section devoted to a thorough discussion of a significant issue, which may lead to a decision at that meeting or at a later one. Some large boards break into smaller groups for this type of discussion and, upon reconvening, report out a summary of their group's conversation and conclusions to the total board. Using different discussion methods and educational styles can add energy to board meetings. (See p. 174 for a sample agenda.)

Boards do need to have reports in order to accomplish their business, but there are methods to get the information to the board without tying up board meetings and wasting valuable time at the meetings.

◆ Mail minutes and reports in advance of the meeting.

◆ Only allow for questions on the reports or brief updates on critical activities or developments since the reports were mailed.

◆ Discuss reports that require action and act on the report's recommendations.

◆ Do not "accept" or "approve" a report. Those two words mean the same thing, and when a board makes such a motion, they are saying that they agree with every word in the report and certify the report's accuracy. This is particularly critical with financial reports. It is only after the annual independent audit that a board can be assured that the figures are accurate, and they then can approve the audit report.

It is part of your responsibilities as a trustee to be sure you have the information you need to make reasoned decisions. Is it clear? Is there too much data? Too little? On target or missing critical items? The written information needs of boards that meet three or four times a year mandate an effective means of communication between meetings.

Some other hints for effective board meetings:

◆ A skilled board chair makes all the difference. If the board chair is not experienced in running meetings or lacks knowledge of parliamentary procedure, find a mentor or "tutor" to assist with chair-training. The committee on trustees can require this step of potential chairs and should discover resources to meet this need.

◆ Group action items together and separate them from discussion items. This helps the board get through the necessary matters efficiently and leaves ample time for issue discussion — the part that trustees value the most.

◆ A board should adopt expectations that establish trustee behavior at meetings, including candor, respect, individual ownership of one's opinions, active participation in discussions, confidentially, etc.

◆ Trustees need to have a basic knowledge of parliamentary procedures. Parliamentary procedure protects the rights of the minority to be heard and the majority to make decisions. (See end of chapter for a simple guide to parliamentary procedure.)

◆ A calendar of the board's work needs to be established, along with a process to bring committee recommendations to the board in a timely manner.

◆ Start and end on time. Schedule the amount of time necessary to accomplish the agenda — no more, no less.

◆ Use a timed agenda. Times can be changed during the meeting by consent or a formal vote of the board.

◆ Make sure that the minutes work for the board. Some ways to improve minutes are:

> Do not record debate, unless a general sense of the issues will explain the actions taken at the meeting or will inform future actions.

> Capitalize, boldface, or underline "motion" so that it is easy to find motions within the body of the minutes. Do likewise with "motion carried" or "motion defeated."

Attach full reports to the official minutes and send any reports given out at the meeting to those who were absent.

Give motions in writing to the secretary to assure accuracy.

Have a cover page summary listing all the major actions of the meeting.

Put the notice of the next meeting at the top of the summary page or on the first page of the minutes.

Have the secretary put her/his name and title at the end of the minutes. According to parliamentary procedure, never use the words "respectfully submitted." If the secretary is not respectful, then he/she should not be the secretary! Once the board has approved the minutes, the secretary should sign the official copy.

Some boards have staff actually take the minutes, and then the secretary, and sometimes the chair, would review them before they are sent to the board. Even in this case, the secretary would sign the official copy.

Board Meeting Frequency and Length

❖ *We meet every month for an hour and a half and still can't finish the agenda!*

Two other frequently asked questions are, "How often should boards meet?" and "How long should the meetings last?" The answer to both is, "That depends." The number of meetings should be based on the type of school (boarding schools meet less frequently than most day schools) and on the organizational structure of the board (those with more committees often meet less frequently than those that do much of their work gathered as the full board.) The typical day school board meets in the evening over the course of nine to ten months a year. About one-third of all schools meet three to four times a year, with boarding schools at the lower end of the range.

The length of board meetings also depends on the type of school. Most boarding school boards come together for one to two days, combining committee and board meetings during that time period. The actual time spent by boarding school trustees in the board meeting can be longer than day schools, where board meetings range from one to four hours. Committee meetings should be based on the same principles as board meetings. However, these meetings tend to be more informal, and the recording of committee actions can be in the form of notes, rather than minutes. Formal motions should be recorded. Remember, committees should schedule their meetings so that their recommendations which need board action can come to the board in a timely manner before the board meeting.

Board Officers

The final ingredient in the recipe of excellent governance is the caliber of the leaders of the leaders — the officers of the board. All trustees are leaders of the school and are equally responsible for the school. Officers agree to assume additional duties in order to facilitate board work. They are not coronated or elevated to some lofty state. They are the servants of the board. The important characteristics of officers can be found in Chapter 6.

Each school's bylaws should state the major responsibilities for each officer in a very brief form. Full job descriptions should be developed for each position and reviewed every few years. The following are meant to be the starting point for such descriptions.

◆ **Chair (President)** is the chief volunteer officer. She/he

Works in partnership with the head in achieving the school's mission and presents a united front to the world-at-large.

Manages the board and coordinates its work, in collaboration with the executive committee.

Develops board and executive committee agendas, in collaboration with the head.

Presides at board and executive committee meetings.

Appoints chairs of committees, with the approval of the executive committee, when required to do so by the bylaws.

Serves ex-officio on all committees and task groups, but does not need to attend every meeting. Chooses to attend the critical committee meetings (i.e., committee on trustees, finance, and strategic planning) or committees that are considering important issues at their meetings.

Plays a leading, visible role in fund development activities, including asking board members for their financial contributions.

Assumes major responsibility in the evaluation of the head.

Represents the board at internal and external events.

Acts as the chief cheerleader for the school and its students.

◆ **Vice Chair (Vice President).** On some boards there is more than one vice chair. The vice chair can:

Preside over board and executive committee meetings in the absence of the chair.

Represent the school at internal and external events in the absence of the chair.

Assumes other responsibilities as assigned by the chair, including chairing a committee.

Coordinate the work of the committees as an alternative that will free up the chair to focus on leading the whole board, fund-raising, and working with the head.

NOTE: *Some schools have the officer position of chair-elect. This person usually has the same responsibility as a vice chair, with the added expectation that she/he would become the chair at the conclusion of the current chair's term.*

◆ **Secretary.** This officer is responsible for board and executive meeting minutes. As noted above some schools have staff take the actual minutes during the meeting, but the secretary of the board is ultimately responsible for the content of the minutes. In the absence of the secretary at a meeting, the chair can appoint a secretary pro-tem. The secretary should examine previous minutes in order to see if there is any unfinished business and, if there is, brings such business to the attention of the chair for inclusion on the agenda of the next meeting. In many jurisdictions, the secretary must sign legal documents in compliance with local statutes.

◆ **Treasurer.** The treasurer of the board interprets the organization's financial information to the board; surfaces financial issues for board consideration; chairs the finance committee unless another trustee fulfills this function; facilitates the committee's development of policies and the budget; and leads its monitoring of budgeted income and expenses.

Note: Some boards have bylaws that give an inaccurate description of the treasurer's duties. Remember, the treasurer is not the school's chief financial officer, business manager, or even the bookkeeper.

As a trustee, you are a member of the leadership team that is the board. You work collegially with other trustees and the head to achieve the board's agenda. You serve on at least one committee or task force and accept assignments as best you can within your time constraints. Remember, if you agree to serve as a trustee, you not only need to make the school a priority in your financial giving, it must be a priority in your commitment of time. When asked, you embrace service as an officer, knowing that this is a special opportunity to contribute your talents to the school for which you are the guardian.

CASE STUDY

Resisting Self-Evaluation

The board of The Thompson School has reviewed the school's most recent accreditation report and has noted with particular interest the comments of the visiting committee under the Governance section. "We recommend," the committee noted, "that the board of trustees consider creating a process of annual self-evaluation to complement its annual evaluation of the head of school." The chair brings this recommendation to the full board for discussion, but the first responses from the floor include comments such as, "How can we evaluate the work of volunteers? We — they — give much to the school, of time and money and other resources." "It would not be fair to evaluate them." "We might lose their interest and support."

The head and chair both join in the conversation, noting that both national and local independent school organizations, as well as the National Center for Nonprofit Boards, recommend that the board regularly evaluate itself and its own leadership, and evaluate the head. But as the meeting adjourns, with agreement that the topic will be revisited at the next meeting, it is obvious that the recommendation did not sit well with a significant portion of the board.

What are the issues?

What should the chair do?

What should the head do?

SAMPLE MATERIALS
Sample Board Meeting Agenda
Call to Order
(Welcome by the chair, who also shares the objectives of the meeting and reviews the agenda.)

Consent Calendar ***
(This is a device to shorten meetings. The items on this calendar are passed by consent (without a vote, if there is no objection) or by formal vote. Single items can be taken off the calendar and considered separately, if even only one member wishes to do so. Typical items on this calendar are:
◆ Minutes
◆ Routine ratification
◆ Board approval required by the bylaws, such as the approval of banking relations.)

Treasurer's Report ***
(This is an opportunity for the treasurer to answer questions on financial reports or bring items for action.)

Head's Report ***
(Opportunity for trustees to ask questions on the written report and for the head to share confidential items she/he did not want to put in writing. The head can also use this time to update trustees on broad educational issues and trends.)

Committee Reports***
(Begin with committees which have action items, then allow time for questions on the other committees' reports. Remember, committees do not need to be on every agenda, if they have not sent out a report or have action items.)

Issues Discussion/In-Depth Board Education ***
(This is the part of the agenda where the board can break up into smaller groups or have interactive education or training.)

Old (Unfinished) Business
(Items that have been postponed from or not finished at previous meetings are handled here.)

New Business
(This is an opportunity for any trustee to bring up items that have not been placed on the agenda. However, it is not a good practice for board members to bring up major issues at this time because there likely would not be enough time for a thorough discussion of the item. Besides which most board members, and certainly the chair and head, do not like surprises!)

Evaluation of the Meeting
(This can be a two minute quick appraisal. Board answers two questions: "What went well?" and "What did not?")

Adjournment

*** *Materials sent to trustees in advance of the board meeting*

A TRUSTEE SURVIVAL KIT

Patrick F. Bassett, president of the Independent Schools Association of the Central States (ISACS), offers the following list of items each trustee should have. It comes from the ISACS "Trustee Handbook/Board Policies Book."

1. School mission statement

2. Brief history of the school

3. Directories: trustee, faculty, parent/student

4. Board committees: structure, charges, assignments

5. Calendars: school year, board and committee meetings

6. Budget/audit

7. Endowment report

8. Strategic plan

9. NAIS *Principles of Good Practice* (complete set)

10. Bylaws

11. Admission catalog and application package

12. School placement profile

13. School statistics (enrollment, financial operations, annual giving, tuition, salaries, etc.)

14. Copy of NAIS *Trustee Handbook*

15. Minutes from last year

16. Board policies: endowment, conflict of interest, nondiscrimination, harassment, financial aid, admission, staffing and personnel, board resolutions, etc.

17. Copy of handbooks: employee and parent/student

18. Board orientation procedures and schedule

PARLIAMENTARY PROCEDURE
AT A GLANCE

To do this	Say...
Adjourn the meeting*	"I move that we adjourn."
Recess the meeting	"I move that we recess until..."
Complain about room temp, etc.*	"Question of privilege."
Suspend further consideration of something*	"I move that the motion be laid on the table."
End debate	"I move the previous question."
Postpone consideration of something*	"I move to postpone this matter until..."
Have something studied further	"I move to refer the motion to the committee."
Amend a motion	"I move that..."
Introduce business (a primary motion)	
Object to procedure or to a personal affront*	"Point of order."
Request information*	"Point of information."
Ask for a vote by actual count to verify a voice vote*	"I call for a division."
Object to considering consideration of some undiplomatic matter*	"I object to the consideration of the question."
Take up a matter previously tabled	"I move to take from the table."
Reconsider something already disposed of	"I move to reconsider." +
Consider something out of its scheduled order*	"I move we suspend the rules and consider..."
Vote on a ruling by the chair*	"I appeal from the decision of the chair."

176
* Not amendable
+ Motion can only be made by someone on the previously prevailing side.

May you interrupt the speaker?	Must you be seconded?	Is the motion debatable?	What vote is required?
No	Yes	No	Majority
No	Yes	No	Majority
Yes	No	No	No Vote
No	Yes	No	Majority
No	Yes	Yes	2/3 Vote
No	Yes	Yes	Majority
No	Yes	Yes	Majority
No	Yes	Yes	Majority
No	Yes	Yes	Majority
Yes	No	No	Chair decides
Yes	No	No	No vote
No	No	No	No vote
Yes	No	No	No vote
No	Yes	No	Majority
Yes	Yes	Yes	Majority
No	Yes	Yes	2/3 Vote
Yes	Yes	Yes	Majority

RESOURCES

Carver, John, *Boards that Make a Difference*, Jossey-Bass, San Francisco, CA, 1997.

Carver, John and Miriam Mayhew Carver, *Reinventing Your Board — A Step-by-Step Guide to Implementing Policy Governance*, Jossey-Bass, San Francisco, CA, 1997.

Chait, Richard P., *How to Help Your Board Govern More and Manage Less*, National Center for Nonprofit Boards, Washington, DC, 1993.

Chait, Richard P., *The Effective Board of Trustees*, American Council on Education/Oryx Series on Higher Education, Washington, DC, 1996.

Ingram, Richard T., *Ten Basic Responsibilities of Nonprofit Boards*, National Center for Nonprofit Boards, Washington, DC, 1996.

O'Connell, Brian, *Board Overboard — Laughs and Lessons for All But the Perfect Nonprofit*, Jossey-Bass, San Francisco, CA, 1995.

Principles of Good Practice for Independent Schools, National Association of Independent Schools, Washington, DC.

Taylor, Barbara E., Richard Chait, and Thomas P. Holland, "The New Work of the Board," *Harvard Business Review*, September-October, 1996.

CHAPTER ELEVEN

Performing the Role of Trustees

To love what you do and feel that it matters — how can anything be more fun?
— *Katharine Graham*

As a trustee, you manage a multitude of roles, assignments, and relationships with good humor and good sense. At times the hours in your day are never sufficient and your finances seem stretched to the limit, and yet you continue your commitment to the school. It must be a very special place!

Scattered throughout this handbook are many specific responsibilities and actions required of trustees as they exercise their governance role. How can you, a trustee, perform this distinctive role with integrity? It begins with understanding what it truly means to hold the school in trust and then how you should conduct yourself in all of your roles and relationships.

Trustees have legal and financial responsibilities for the school, but as trustholders they have a much deeper attachment to the school — its mission, students, and faculty. Trustees have a profound understanding of the school's character and identity, champion it as it is now, and visualize what it can be in the future. Their connection to the school is deep and personal.

Duties of Care, Loyalty, and Obedience

❖ Haven't I got enough duties as it is?

There are certain standards that trustees must meet in their conduct as they fulfill their responsibilities. Often they are described as the duties of care, loyalty, and obedience.

The Duty of Care

The duty of care describes the level of competence expected of a trustee. State nonprofit corporate laws have various definitions of this duty in suitable "legalese," but they all come down to the importance of trustees making good decisions with reasonable care. Trustees do not need to make perfect decisions; they do not need to be experts in child development and education. However, they need to recognize that they should hire people to provide the necessary wisdom, skill, and expertise to enact the school's program and mission and to set up policies and procedures to avoid risks to the school's financial well-being and the health and safety of its students and staff.

The Duty of Loyalty

The duty of loyalty is the standard of faithfulness to the school. A trustee must put the school first when making decisions. This duty is the basis for conflict of interest policies that are designed to prevent board members from enriching themselves and their families and friends at the expense of the school, as well as favoring one segment of the school over another. There is more on conflicts of interest later in this chapter.

The Duty of Obedience

The duty of obedience requires trustees to be true to the school's mission. Board members can exercise their own reasoned judgment in how the school can best achieve its mission. They cannot act in a manner that is inconsistent with that mission. This duty is based on the fact that the school's constituents and the public-at-large act in reliance that what they are told is true about the school. If there is a discrepancy between the trustees' understanding of the school's mission and goals and that of the head, the results can be disastrous for all involved with the school. If the disconnection is between the trustees and the school's constituents and the public at large, the result is the loss of institutional integrity — another form of disaster.

Conflict of Interest

❖ If I have all of these duties, how can I protect myself?

Trustees tend to be active, involved, and influential people, most of whom are deeply connected to the school and are sought for just those reasons. However, this means that they have some loyalties that can be in competition with each other and with the school and their colleagues. In Chapter 1 there is a brief description of the role of board members in identifying and managing any conflicts of interest they may have. The board and individual trustees can take steps to assure that every trustee fulfills his or her obligation to separate personal interests from those of the school. For trustees, the school comes first.

Boards can:

◆ Adopt a conflict of interest policy that enjoins trustees or their family members from gaining financial or personal advantage from their board service. This policy should be drafted by legal counsel and adopted by the board.(See p. 188 for a sample policy.)

◆ Ask every trustee to sign an annual statement that acknowledges that they understand the conflicts of interest policy and to list any current or potential conflict they have that could involve their board work.

◆ Orient new trustees to the conflict of interest policy and how it plays out in practice. Give examples of the type of conflicts typically found within independent school boards.

◆ Have periodic discussions at board meetings on why the conflict of interest policy protects the school and all trustees from being involved improperly in board decisions. These discussions can also help the school from being perceived as an institution whose trustees can better their personnel and financial situations by their board service. This conversation can be especially appropriate when setting tuitions with parent-trustees on the board.

◆ Establish a tradition that the board will deal openly on all matters that come before it.

◆ Hire an outside investment manager for the endowment funds; have a yearly financial audit by an independent auditor; and require an independent appraisal of any property given to the school.

◆ Establish a policy that all major contracts for goods and services will be put out to bid.

Trustees can:

◆ Sign the annual statement that they understand the conflict of interest policy and list all current and potential conflicts; if you are not sure what constitutes a conflict, consult the chair, who may put you in touch with school's counsel.

◆ Be conscious of any conflicts that may arise after making the list and bring them to the attention of the chair.

◆ If a conflict does arise, make sure the board knows what the situation is and recuse yourself from the discussion and vote. Make sure that the minutes reflect this action.

◆ Always keep board discussions and decisions confidential, including those whose disclosure might benefit a relative, friend, or business associate.

◆ Whenever you are not sure if one of your biases is coloring your approach to a problem or decision, ask yourself, "What must the board do that is in the best interest of the school as a whole?" Not every trustee will agree on the specific answer to that question, but it will keep everyone focused on their trustee role as keeper of the mission for the total school.

The success of avoiding conflicts of interest depends upon the board developing policies and following them rigorously and encouraging open discussion on all issues. Such success also depends on the ability of individual trustees to govern themselves with integrity and to hold the school in trust. Not to do so can open the board and individual members up to lawsuits alleging that their self-interest has harmed the school, which unfortunately can be true. Above all, the abrogation of the duty of loyalty can create distrust and ruin the morale of the board, head, and staff — not to mention that of the students, parents, and alumnae/i.

Other Standards of Conduct

What are some of the other standards of behavior that are evidenced by
effective trustees who truly serve as guardians of the school? The following
amplifies the subject matter of Chapter 1 and its focus on *Principles of Good
Practice for Independent School Trustees.*

Good principles for good practice

❖ *You mean
I need to
speak out?*

Trustees are expected to support the school's mission and the resulting strategic plan and to give and get funds that assist the fulfillment of the mission
and plan. How should they do it? They need to be visible in all of their various activities, since they are models for the school community. Their financial
contributions should be among the earliest given, at the highest level their
circumstances allow, and done with good cheer. Their responses to questions
about the school should be honest and as positive as possible, and their commitment to the plan should be demonstrated through active participation in
activities that further the plan. They should seek out formal and informal
opportunities to spread the word about the wonderful school they serve.
Trustees inspire others to believe in the school and to support it with their
time, expertise, and funds.

Accepting responsibility for the boards' effectiveness

❖ *The board
is not a
quarterly
tea party!*

Trustees exercise their major governance responsibilities through collective
actions, which occur at board meetings. Just showing up to the meeting is
the first step, but it is only the beginning. Trustees need to be aware that they
are responsible for board decisions, whether they are present or not. In fact,
if trustees vote "no" on an issue, they are still liable if it goes forward, unless
they get their names recorded in the minutes as voting against the motion or
writing a letter to indicate their opposition. While the board chair is charged
with presiding at board meetings, board members need to accept responsibility for the effectiveness of the meetings. They do this by:

◆ Keeping the school's mission as the basis of all major decisions. (Putting
the mission statement on the wall of the room where board meetings are
held can help trustees focus on the major priorities that stem from that
mission.)

◆ Actively listening to others.

◆ Owning their opinions and stating them succinctly.

◆ Staying on point in their statements and encouraging others to do likewise.

◆ Asking clarifying questions.

◆ Knowing parliamentary procedure and using it when it can further the board's work.

◆ Assisting the members of the board to reach a conclusion, knowing that not to decide is a decision.

Trustees should exhibit this same behavior beyond the board table at committee meetings and other school gatherings.

True commitment

❖ *You mean I do need to show up?*

Remember, when trustees are chronically absent from meetings, the board loses their expertise and wisdom. This subverts the very reason they were elected to the board. Board chairs need to counsel such delinquent members, assuring them they are missed, learning if they feel disengaged and why, and asking them to consider other ways than board service to demonstrate their commitment to the school.

Complete support for board decisions

❖ *How can I support that decision? I didn't vote for it!*

Once decisions have been made by the board, trustees have the duty of loyalty — that is to support the decisions once they become "public," even when in opposition to it. This circumstance does not arise often, but when it does, trustees find it very stressful. However, if the board's deliberations leading to the adoption of the proposal were informed and thoughtful, "losing" trustees may be comforted by the fact that every board member understood the question, had the school's best interests at heart, and still valued them as full members of the board. The majority just did not agree with the minority! If the matter is of such great importance that the opposing trustees cannot support the conclusion in public, they need to resign. The number of times such resignations occur is very few, but boards should not rescind previous decisions to appease a few unhappy trustees who may threaten to resign, especially if a strong majority believes the action was right.

Confidentiality

Another trustee obligation is to keep all discussions and decisions confidential until, if ever, the board determines it is appropriate for the information to leave the board room. The issue of confidentiality runs throughout this handbook because it is so critical to the effective functioning of the board. "Secrecy" sounds so negative in an open society, but there are topics and circumstances that require it. It may be a matter of timing, as when a board begins a preliminary examination of major changes in a school. (Ex: adding to the faculty workload, acquisition of a neighboring property, going coeducational, etc.) It can be the actual subject matter itself that requires stringent confidence. (Ex: discontent with the head's performance, negative self-assessment of the board's performance, allegations of a massive student drug problem, etc.)

Trustee standards

Much of what has been stated in this handbook makes it appear as if trustees have to be perfect in order to serve their school effectively. If that was true, there would be no one capable of governing and leading the school. The standards for trustee performance need to be high because boards only want the best for their schools and that includes the best trustees. Remember, it is through the collective expertise, wisdom, and actions of board members that good governance occurs. Individual trustees may find themselves in different places during their time of service, capable of giving more time or treasure at one time and less at another. Trustees are human after all. However, there can be no compromise over the commitment to the school's mission, observation of the duties of care, loyalty, and obedience, and the basic integrity of all trustees.

Fundamental Questions

As a trustee, you are responsible for your own actions and opinions. You dedicate yourself to working diligently and thoughtfully for the school through your governance role.

You ask yourself three fundamental questions throughout your trusteeship:

◆ Do I add value to the work and life of the board and to the school?

◆ Am I learning from my experiences, both those from my work and board educational opportunities, and improving my effectiveness?

◆ Am I having fun?

If the answer is not "yes" to all three questions, then trusteeship may not be for you. Never forget that you are the guardian of the well-being of the school of today and tomorrow. You are a trustholder.

CASE STUDY

Bounds of the Board Authority

Over spring break, parents of two of School X's students filed a sexual harassment suit on behalf of their children against the board and against Tim Davis, a popular coach. The suit alleges that board members knowingly created a hostile climate for female students in two ways: 1) by retaining Davis after one allegation of harassment against him was filed (and ultimately dismissed in court), and 2) by failing to fully and properly investigate all such charges against faculty. Lawyers for the board contend that it is not the responsibility of board members to constitute an investigatory body for charges of harassment, and that such investigations should be left to the proper authorities.

What are the issues?

What should the board do?

What should the board chair do?

What should the head do?

SAMPLE MATERIALS

Sample Conflict of Interest Statement for Board of Trustees

The Board of Trustees are appointed/elected to serve [Name of School] and its constituencies. The men and women who accept this position are expected to carry out their duties in a manner which inspires and assures the confidence of the school and the broader community.

The Trustees shall exercise the utmost good faith in all transactions touching upon their duties to the organization and its property. In their dealings with and on behalf of the organization, they are held to a strict rule of honest and fair dealing between themselves and the organization. They shall not use their positions as Trustees, or knowledge gained therefrom, so that a conflict might arise between the school's interest and that of any individual Trustee.

A conflict of interest arises in any situation in which a Trustee (and his or her immediate family) is involved in an activity which could adversely affect his or her judgment with respect to the business of the school or otherwise diminish the interest of the organization. When such a conflict arises, the individual with the conflict is expected to disclose in writing the existence of the conflict.

RESOURCES

Andringa, Robert C. and Ted W. Engstrom, *Nonprofit Board Answer Book, Practical Guidelines for Board Members and Chief Executives*, National Center for Nonprofit Boards, Washington, DC, 1997.

Carver, John, Miram Mayhew Carver, *Reinventing Your Board, A Step-by-Step Guide to Implementing Policy Governance*. Jossey-Bass, San Francisco, 1997.

Principles of Good Practice for Independent School Trustees, National Association of Independent Schools, Washington, DC., 1997 (part of a complete set of Principles of Good Practice for Independent Schools).

Greenleaf, Robert, Don M. Frick, Larry C. Spears, Editors, *On Becoming a Servant Leader — The Private Writings of Robert K. Greenleaf,* Jossey-Bass, San Francisco, CA, 1996.

Leifer, Jacqueline Covey and Michael B. Glomb, *Legal Obligations of Nonprofit Boards — A Guidebook for Board Members,* National Center for Nonprofit Boards, Washington, DC, 1997.

APPENDIX 1

The following is a list of organizations, publications, and websites that can be of help to independent school trustees. Many of the organizations listed provide services for members only. Some offer workshops that are open to nonmembers. Others provide consulting services for a fee.

Organizations:

Alumni Program Council for Independent Schools
3515 Leeds Road
Cleveland, OH 44122-4261
216-464-3306
www.apcnetwork.org

This well-established organization plans an annual series of workshops across the country. Offers a newsletter and other resources for alumni programs.

Association of Governing Boards of Universities and Colleges
One Dupont Circle Suite 400, NW
Washington, DC 20036
202-296-8400
www.agb.org

Dedicated to strengthening the performance of boards of public and private higher education; offers workshops and resource publications.

Council for the Advancement and Support of Education

1307 New York Avenue, NW
Suite 1000
Washington, DC 20005-4701
202-328-5900
www.case.org

CASE supports a wide range of advancement and development programs for 4 year colleges, 2 year colleges, and secondary schools. Each winter, they host the major conference: CASE/NAIS.

Educational Directions Incorporated

P.O. Box 768
Portsmouth, RI 02871
401-683-3523
www.ediwsii.com

A consulting firm offering newsletters by subscription, including the Trustee's Letter and the Head's Letter.

Harvard Business School

Executive Education Programs
Soldiers Field - Glass House
Boston, MA 02163-9986
1-800-HBS-5577 ext. 7011
www.exed.hbs.edu

Often in conjunction with the Graduate School of Education, the Business School offers a variety of programs, workshops, and the Harvard Business Review, all useful leadership and management resources.

Independent School Chairmen Association

3670 Beacon Street
Boston, MA 02116
617-236-8794

A membership organization for board chairs in independent schools. Holds several annual programs.

Independent School Management

1316 North Union Street
Wilmington, DE 19806
302-656-4944
www.isminc.com

A research, analysis, and consulting firm devoted to the management needs of independent schools. Produces two advisory publications, Ideas & Perspectives and To the Point; offers administrative workshops.

NACUBO
2501 M Street NW Suite 400
Washington, DC 20037-1308
202-861-2500
www.nacubo.org

A nonprofit professional organization representing chief administrative and financial officers at more than 2,100 colleges and universities across the country.

National Association of Independent Schools
1620 L Street, NW
Washington, DC 20036
202-973-9700
www.nais-schools.org

A voluntary membership organization for over 1,100 member schools and associations in the United States and abroad, and the national institutional advocate for independent precollegiate education.

National Center for Nonprofit Boards
2000 L Street, NW Suite 510
Washington, DC 20036-4907
202-452-6262
www.ncnb.org

Serving a broad range of nonprofit organizations, the NCNB, in addition to planning an annual conference each fall, offers and updates a number of monographs in areas to help boards improve.

General Newsletters/Magazines:

Independent School, NAIS, Washington, DC (by subscription)

Leadership Forum, NAIS, Washington, DC (for members only)

The Head's Letter, Educational Directions, Inc. Portsmouth, RI

The Trustee's Letter, Educational Directions, Inc. Portsmouth, RI

Ideas and Perspectives, ISM, Wilmington, DE

Nonprofit Board Report, National Center for Nonprofit Boards, Washington, DC

Board Member, National Center for Nonprofit Boards, Washington, DC

Key Websites

Alumni Program Council — www.apcnetwork.org

Association of Governing Boards — www.agb.org

Harvard Business School — www.exed.hbs.edu

Independent School Association of the Central States — www.isacs.org

National Association of Independent Schools — www.nais-schools.org
(Note: The NAIS website is hyperlinked to member local, state, and regional
association sites.)

APPENDIX 2

Parliamentary Glossary

Ad hoc — A Latin term meaning "for this case alone" and used to designate a special or short-term committee.

Agenda — An outline of the order of business for use by the chair and the board during a meeting.

Amend — Modify, change, or improve a motion before it is adopted or rejected.

Are you ready for the question? — Debate discussion is now in order.

Announcing the vote — Declaration by the chair of the result of the vote.

Authority (Parliamentary) — The authority adopted by an assembly to govern parliamentary procedure during its meetings, usually Roberts Rules of Order, Newly Revised.

Aye and No — Terms used in voice voting. "Aye" is pronounced "I."

Budget — An itemized estimate of income and expenses.

Bylaws — A document, adopted by the board or a society, which contains the basic rules for governing that board or organization.

Call for the Orders of the Day — A motion used to call for a return to the scheduled order of business.

Carried — Same as adopted. (A motion is "carried.")

Chair — The presiding officer. Authority is vested in the office, not in the person.

Commit — To place a proposition in the hands of a committee.

Division of the Assembly — The motion calls for a rising vote.

Division of the Question — Separating a motion in two or more distinct parts for the purpose of debating and voting upon each part separately.

Ex-Officio — By virtue of office. The bylaws often provide that the chair is an ex-officio member of all committees. Must be notified of all meetings, has voice and vote but is not included in the quorum. To deny an ex-officio member a vote, the bylaws should state that the individual serves "ex-officio without a vote."

General Consent — Informal agreement of the assembly. A form of voting in which there is no dissenting vote. "If there is no objection..."

Germane — Closely related; of the same subject matter. Example: An amendment must be germane to the motion to which it is applied.

Illegal Vote — A vote which can not be credited to any candidate or choice but which is counted in determining the number of votes cast for the purpose of computing the majority.

Immediate Pending Questions — The last question stated by the chair when several questions are pending, sometimes called the "last pending question."

Incidental Motions — Those which arise out of a pending question rather than from the business itself. Example: Request for information, suspension of the rules, etc.

Main Motion — One that introduces a subject to the assembly for discussion and action.

Majority Vote — More than half of the votes cast by persons legally entitled to vote.

Pending Question — Before the board or assembly. A question is pending from the time it is stated by the chair until it is disposed of, either temporarily or permanently.

Plurality Vote — The largest portion of the votes cast when there are more than two choices. A plurality vote never decides a question or constitutes an election except by specific rule of the board or organization.

Precedence — Priority in order or rank in which motions are considered and acted on.

Precedent — An established custom or preceding instance or case that may serve as an example or justification in future similar cases, in the absence of a rule.

Previous Question — Motion to close debate and take the vote at once on the immediately pending question. Vote is first on closing debate, and if the vote passes, the board immediately (without any further debate) votes on the pending question. If the vote does not carry, debate on the pending question continues.

Pro Tem — Temporarily; usually applied to one who serves in the absence of a regular officer or chair of a committee.

Quroum — The number of members required to be present so that the assembly may transact business. The quorum is a majority of all members, unless the bylaws state otherwise.

Ratify — An incidental main motion to approve action already taken, but which requires a vote of the board or assembly to make the action valid.

Rescind — To annul some action of the board or assembly previously taken.

Revision of Bylaws — A complete set of bylaws submitted as a substitute for existing bylaws.

Seriatum — Considered by paragraph.

Sine Die — "Without a Day." Adjournment without a time set for the next meeting, as in a convention.

Standing Rules — Rules of temporary or semi-permanent nature, relating to detail of the administration; remain in force until amended or rescinded.

Tie Vote — Less than a majority. (A motion is lost when there is a tie vote. The chair may vote to break a tie, but if the matter is of major importance, the chair needs to be very sure that it is the right thing to do for the board at that time.)

Two-third Vote — Two out of three votes cast. Example: For two-third approval the affirmative vote is at least twice as large as the negative.

Unfinished Business — Matters on the agenda of a previous meeting on which no action was taken.

Viva Voce — Voice vote. All those in favor say, "aye." All those opposed say, "no."

Withdraw a Motion — To remove a motion from consideration by the board or assembly upon request by the mover, and by permission of the board or assembly if the motion has been stated by the chair.

INDEX

ABOUT THE AUTHOR

Mary Hundley DeKuyper is a former trustee of The Bryn Mawr School (Maryland) where she was president of the board (1984-1988) and of the alumnae association (1980-1982). She was a member and chair of the Association of Independent Maryland Schools' trustee committee. Mary has chaired eleven other nonprofit boards and served on an additional eight. She is a graduate of The Bryn Mawr School and Wellesley College. She combines her avocation, service on boards, with her vocation, consulting with nonprofits, with an emphasis on governance concerns. Many of her clients are independent schools and private and public institutions of higher education. Mary is associated with the National Center for Nonprofit Boards, the Association of Governing Boards of Universities and Colleges, and the Venetian Group.

To order more copies of this book,
go to *www.nais.org*
or order from 1-800-793-6701 or 301-396-5911.